COMPASS: COMPUTER APPLICATION SOFTWARE SERIES
Dennis P. Curtin, Series Editor

dBASE IV®
A Short Course

Dennis P. Curtin

 Prentice Hall, Englewood Cliffs, New Jersey 07632

Editorial/production supervision: *bookworks*
Interior design: Christine Gehring-Wolf
Cover design: Lundgren Graphics
Manufacturing buyer: Peter Havens

Printed in the United States of America
10 9 8 7 6 5 4 3 2 1

ISBN 0-13-199738-6

Prentice-Hall International (UK) Limited, *London*
Prentice-Hall of Australia Pty, Limited, *Sydney*
Prentice-Hall Canada Inc., *Toronto*
Prentice-Hall Hispanoamericana, S.A., *Mexico*
Prentice-Hall of India Private Limited, *New Delhi*
Prentice-Hall of Japan, Inc., *Tokyo*
Simon & Schuster Asia Pte. Ltd., *Singapore*
Editora Prentice-Hall do Brasil, Ltda, *Rio de Janeiro*

Contents

PART II   PROJECTS   141

Preface

▼RATIONALE

This text has been designed to provide you with an introductory background in working with dBASE IV®. It does so by introducing you to the program on three levels: concepts, procedures, and activities.

CONCEPTS

Concepts are discussed because they provide the background for procedures. They explain principles, all of which apply to dBASE IV, but many of which also apply to other programs you will use on a microcomputer. When you understand concepts, procedures are easier to learn because they fit into a framework. Understanding concepts also makes it much easier to transfer your understanding to other programs, and other computers.

PROCEDURES

Procedures are the specific skills one has to know to use dBASE IV. They include such fundamental steps as saving a file, or making a printout. To work with a program, you have to understand more than one procedure because you almost always want to save your work and make printouts to share with others. In this sense procedures are like individual bricks, that when joined together make larger structures like arches, walls, and bridges. Some procedures are generally considered to be more advanced than others, and the organization of the procedures in this manual follows those conventions. This conventional classification of procedures into introductory and advanced can be misleading however. Many procedures considered to be advanced are really quite simple, and very useful. Although procedures in this text are presented in a sequence from simple to complex, don't hesitate to study the advanced procedures. You'll find many of them easy to use and quite exciting.

ACTIVITIES

Concepts and procedures tell you why to do something and how to do it, but they don't tell you what to do it with. To gain that knowledge, concepts and procedures have to be put to work in real-world situations. To fulfill this goal, many tutorials, exercises, and projects have been included in this text. These activities serve more than one purpose.

- They build skills in the specific procedures you need to know.
- They demonstrate a variety of situations in which specific procedures are useful.
- They introduce important business, and other, principles that have been, or will be, introduced in other courses in the curriculum.
- They develop problem-solving skills. Exercises provide less help than tutorials, and projects provide even less. Moving through this sequence of activities challenges you to think about what you should do, and why you need to do it.

To complete some of these activities, a copy of the *dBASE IV Resource Disk* is required. This disk contains the files needed for optional exercises and for the project at the end of this text. It contains actual U.S. Bureau of the Census files that too large to create yourself but provide useful experience in working with larger real-world databases.

▼ORGANIZATION

This text is designed to be used in a lab-oriented course. It is organized into two parts.

Part I covers the procedures you use to work with dBASE IV and is organized into 14 topics that cover procedures step by step. Each topic has the following elements:

- **Concepts** introduce the basic principles discussed in the topic—the why, when, and where of working with databases.
- **Procedures** describe step by step how you execute commands—the how of working with dBASE IV. This section serves a dual function. You can refer to it when working on the tutorials and exercises in this text or use it as a quick reference when working on your own projects.
- **Tips** in many topics discuss advanced procedures or cross reference you to other topics where related procedures are discussed.
- **Tutorials** demonstrate step by step how to use the procedures discussed in the topic.
- **Exercises** provide you with additional opportunities to practice and gain experience with the concepts and procedures discussed in the topic. Unlike tutorials, exercises do not guide you step by step. You have to determine the correct procedures to use. These exercises have been selected so they are relevant to business and should prove both interesting and challenging.
- **Questions** test your understanding of the concepts and procedures discussed in the topic.

When this text is used in the classroom, all topics do not have to be covered. However, many tutorials and exercises assume that previous tutorials and exercises have already been completed. In these cases, the introduction to the tutorial or exercise cross references you to the tutorial or exercise that must have been completed first.

Part II contains a project that builds skills and introduces problem solving. The project, making marketing decisions based on U.S. Bureau of the Census data, is typical of those that people encounter in school and business. Step by step instructions for the completion of this project are not provided. To complete it, you must first have mastered the procedures listed for the project.

▼THE COMPASS SERIES

This text is part of an integrated series, *Computer Application Software Series,* or *COMPASS*. The texts in this series, like this one, use a standardized approach to introducing operating systems and applications software. Many of the texts in the series are available in two versions: one for complete courses, and one for short courses.

- The complete course versions cover all features of the program and are suitable for a full semester course or where you want extensive coverage of a program.
- The short course versions are adapted from the complete course versions. They are designed to be used in a course where more than one program is being covered or when time is limited and you want to cover only the most important features of the program. They are similar to the complete course versions but contain fewer topics, tutorials, exercises, and projects.

TITLES

The COMPASS series contained the following texts at the time this one was published. Each text covers the latest version of their respective programs.

DOS 4: A Complete Course
WordPerfect 5.0: A Complete Course
Lotus 1-2-3: A Complete Course
dBASE IV: A Complete Course

DOS: A Short Course
WordPerfect 5.0: A Short Course
Lotus 1-2-3: A Short Course
dBASE IV: A Short Course
Telecommunications with ProComm Plus®: A Short Course

These texts are updated as soon as a new version of the program is introduced and previous versions of the text are kept in print as long as there is a demand for them. Also, new titles are introduced when major new programs gain wide acceptance in college and university courses. To obtain an up-to-date listing of the titles in the series, contact your Prentice Hall representative.

SUPPLEMENTS

The publisher has developed many supplements for the COMPASS series that are free on adoption. These supplements include:

- **dBASE IV Resource Disk.** The *dBASE IV Resource Disk* contains the files needed to complete optional exercises and project on analyzing U.S. Census Bureau data. If you do not have this disk, you can obtain a single copy free to use as a master when making copies for your students. To obtain a free copy, contact your local Prentice Hall representative or call Prentice Hall's Software Department toll-free at 1-800-842-2958. Be sure to specify whether the disk should be in the 5¼-inch or 3½-inch format.
- **Instructor's Resource Manual** contains suggested course outlines and teaching suggestions and test questions.
- **Videos** on the programs covered in this series are available to qualified adopters of this text. Contact your local Prentice Hall representative for details.

▼ACKNOWLEDGMENTS

No book is the result of the efforts of a single person. Although the author accepts responsibility for the final results, he was assisted during the development of this text and would like to express his appreciation to the following people.

The first edition of this text was reviewed and commented on by William J. Ferns, Jr., Baruch College; R. Kenneth Walter, Weber State College; Marie-Claire Barthelemy, Norwalk Community College; Lory Hawkes, DeVry Institute of Technology; Elizabeth M. Nilsen, Westbrook College; Beth Cheatham, Central Texas College; Patricia J. McCue, Orlando College; James A. Pope, Old Dominion University; Steven Siegfried, Owens Technical College; and Chris Carter, Indiana Vocational Technical College. All these teachers made many suggestions for improvements, and the book is now better as a result of their efforts.

Peggy Curtin handled all communications with computer companies and coordinated the art program for the series.

Finally, special thanks to Toni M. Hutto of Wake Technical Community College, Raleigh, NC, who tested all the tutorials, exercises, and projects in this text. Her contributions have been enormous, but the author remains solely responsible should any errors or shortcomings remain in the text.

Dennis P. Curtin
Marblehead, Massachusetts

Conventions

This text uses the following conventions for keys (see Table 1), commands, and prompts.

TABLE 1   Key Conventions

Name	IBM Keyboard	This Text
Return or Enter	⏎	**Enter**
Caps lock	Caps Lock	**Caps Lock**
Control	Ctrl	**Ctrl**
Escape	Esc	**Esc**
Function keys	F1 through F10	**F1 through F10**
Home	Home	**Home**
End	End	**End**
Page up	PgUp	**PgUp**
Page down	PgDn	**PgDn**
Delete	Del	**Del**
Backspace	←	**Backspace**
Insert	Ins	**Ins**
Print screen	PrtSc	**PrtSc**
Number lock	Num Lock	**Num Lock**
Scroll lock	Scroll Lock	**Scroll Lock**
Shift	⇧	**Shift**
Space bar	None	**Spacebar**
Alt	Alt	**Alt**
Left arrow	←	←
Right arrow	→	→
Down arrow	↓	↓
Up arrow	↑	↑
Tab	⇥	**Tab**
Backtab	⇤	**Backtab**
Hyphen or Minus sign	-	**Hyphen**
Underscore	▭	**Underscore**
Gray+	+[a]	**Gray+**
Gray—	—[a]	**Gray—**

[a] The **Gray+** and **Gray—** keys are the keys labeled + and — to the right of the numeric keypad.

COMMANDS

- Keys you press sequentially are separated by commas. For example, if you are to press F8, release it, and then press ENTER, the instructions read F8, ENTER.
- Keys you press simultaneously are separated by dashes. For example, if you are to hold down the CTRL key while you press F8, the instructions read CTRL-F8.

PROMPTS

All prompts that appear on the screen are shown *in this typeface*. When a prompt appears, you type a response and then press ENTER. All answers you type in response to prompts are shown in **BOLDFACE**.

SUMMARY

Now that you have read about how keys and commands are presented, see if you can understand the following instructions.

To Open a Database File

1. Highlight the name of the database file in the Control Center's Data panel.
2. Press ENTER to retrieve the file. Its name is listed above the horizontal bar in the panel.

To open a database file that already exists, you highlight its name and then press ENTER.

To Print a Quick Report

1. Highlight the name of the database on the Control Center's Data panel, or display the Browse or Edit screen.
2. Press SHIFT-F9 to display a submenu. (The choices on the menu are discussed in Table 32.)
3. Press B for *Begin printing.*

To print out a quick report, you first move the highlight to the name of the database you want to print. You then hold down the SHIFT key while you press F9. When a menu appears, you press B to begin printing.

I

Procedures

▼ DATABASE MANAGEMENT—AN OVERVIEW

The concept behind database management programs like dBASE IV is simple. They allow you to store information, retrieve it when you need it, and update it when necessary. You can store large amounts of information like mailing lists, inventory records, or billing and collection information in files. You can then manipulate the information in these files with the database management program. For example, you can:

- Add new information
- Find specific information
- Update information that has changed
- Sort the information into a specified order
- Delete information that is no longer needed
- Print out labels and reports containing all or some of the information

The management of databases is one of the most important applications of microcomputers. A database is simply one or more files that contains an organized body of information. The database exists but doesn't actually do anything itself. To create, maintain, and use a database, you use a database management program.

RECORD MANAGEMENT PROGRAMS

In the early days of business computing, separate programs were created for each application. For example, the payroll department would have a program that created and maintained a file containing names, addresses, and payroll information of employees. The personnel department would use a different program that maintained a separate file containing names, addresses, hiring dates, insurance policies, and vacation schedules. Whenever a new application was needed, a new program was written, and the data needed for that application was entered and maintained. The data in the payroll department's file could not be used by the personnel department's program. Each of the files the information was stored in could be used only by the program that created it. If an employee changed her name or left the firm, several files would have to be updated.

 Data vs Datum

The term *data* is one that you frequently encounter when working with databases and other computer programs. It is the plural form of the term *datum.* When you use the term, you should always do so with plural verbs. For example, you would not say "the data *is* inconclusive." Instead, you would say "the data *are* inconclusive."

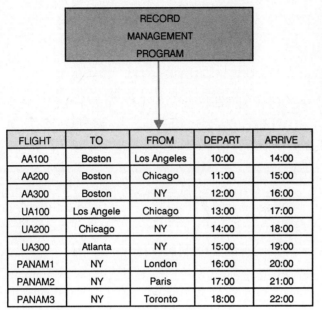

FIGURE 1 Record Management Programs. Record management programs can address only one file at a time. To manage information in another file, you must clear the first file from memory and then retrieve the new one.

Record management programs (sometimes called file management or flat file database programs), are like those integrated into many word processing (Word-Perfect) and spreadsheet (Lotus 1-2-3) programs. These programs store, maintain, and use data stored in single files (Figure 1). If you use a record management program to store data on various aspects of a business, you must store the data for different applications in separate files. If you want to make changes, you must make them in each file when information is duplicated. Let's say you have one file for names, addresses, and phone numbers and another file for payroll information. If a person's name occurs in both files, the name must be separately entered into each file. If the name must be changed or deleted later, it must be separately changed in or deleted from each file.

DATABASE MANAGEMENT PROGRAMS

As the amount of information being processed increases, the record management method of using separate files to store information becomes cumbersome because information must be extensively duplicated. An employee's name might appear in several different files, for example, payroll, vacation, and expense accounts. There are disadvantages to this duplication:

- It increases the risk of errors in the information. Since a person's name would have to be entered more than once, any changes in status would have to be made in different files, perhaps by different people. Over time, the data's accuracy deteriorates. For example, changes might be made in some files and not in others, or some data might be entered correctly into one file and incorrectly into another.
- It increases the amount of data entry since some information must be entered more than once.
- It requires more storage space, which causes problems when the database is large.

The introduction of databases eliminated these problems. In a database, the data are stored so that there is no duplication of data. For example, a person's name can appear in the database only once, so a change must be made only once.

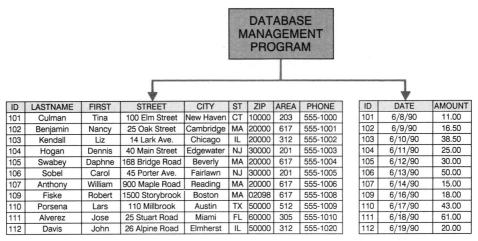

A. NAMELIST File   B. AMOUNTS File

FIGURE 2   Database Management Programs.   Database management programs can manage the data in more than one file.

Database management programs (also called database management systems, or DBMS) are used to manage these databases. They can do everything a record management program can do, but they can also do much more. The main difference is that a database management program can use interrelated data stored in more than one file (Figure 2), thus eliminating the duplication of data and the need to enter updates more than once into different files.

Database management programs, therefore, have a major advantage over record management programs since many applications they are used for require more than one file. For example, the accounting process requires separate files for the general ledger, accounts receivable, and accounts payable. A program that can work with more than one file eliminates the need for duplicating information in separate files and reduces the task of updating the information. Moreover, because data are entered only once, the accuracy of the information is much improved.

DATABASE MODELS

When you enter information into a database, the information is stored on the disk in one or more files. This is the physical storage of the information. Programs that update and manipulate the information in the database handle all aspects of the physical storage so that you do not have to. Although the physical storage is not important to you, the way you view the data, its logical storage, is. Logical storage refers to the way the information in different files can be related.

The logical arrangement of files is called the database model (or database schema). Three typical models are network, hierarchical, and relational. Almost all microcomputer database management programs, including dBASE IV, use the relational model, so this is the only model we discuss in this part.

To understand a relational database, imagine a drawer in a filing cabinet. Information is stored in folders and inserted into the drawer. In a record management system, each set of folders stands alone; thus, to find a specific letter, you select the most likely folder and look in it. If the letter is not there, you try again. But in a relational database, each folder is cross-referenced to other folders in the file. If the letter is not in the first folder, cross-references suggest other files you should look in. In a database, these cross-references are called relationships.

A relational database consists of one or more tables, called relations. These tables, or relations, contain rows and columns much like a spreadsheet (Figure 3).

Since a database can contain more than one table, the tables can be linked to one another (Figure 4). As you see later, you manipulate the data in these tables to enter, update, and find information stored in the database. You can also combine two or more files into a new file.

Before discussing dBASE IV in detail, we look briefly at the procedures you would follow to create and use a database file that contains names and addresses. We discuss all the procedures introduced here in greater detail in the following topics, but this overview should give you a feel for how these programs work and how you can use them.

Step 1: Defining the Database

Once you have a list of the information that you want to store, you create a database file to store it in. This information is not stored randomly in a file; it must be stored in a highly organized way so that the program can find it later. The way data are organized in a database is really quite simple. They are always organized into fields and records (Figure 5):

- A record is a description of a single person, thing, or activity. In this example, a record is the complete name, address, and phone number for a person.
- A field is one part of the description stored in the record. In our file, the name is one field, the address is another field, and the phone number is a third field.

When you first create a database file, you have to tell the program what fields you plan on storing so that it can allocate room for them. This step is called defining the database. When you define a database, you describe each field by specifying its name, type of data to be stored (for example, text, dates, or numbers that can be calculated), and width. You enter these descriptions on the database design screen.

FIGURE 3 Relational Database. A relational database table contains rows and columns much like a spreadsheet.
A. The columns are fields, and the labels at the top of each field are the field names. Each column on the table has a fixed length.
B. There is one or more rows of data, and each row is a record.
C. Each field contains data.

ID	LASTNAME	FIRST	STREET	CITY	ST	ZIP	AREA	PHONE
101	Culman	Tina	100 Elm Street	New Haven	CT	10000	203	555-1000
102	Benjamin	Nancy	25 Oak Street	Cambridge	MA	20000	617	555-1001
103	Kendall	Liz	14 Lark Ave.	Chicago	IL	20000	312	555-1002
104	Hogan	Dennis	40 Main Street	Edgewater	NJ	30000	201	555-1003
105	Swabey	Daphne	168 Bridge Road	Beverly	MA	20000	617	555-1004
106	Sobel	Carol	45 Porter Ave.	Fairlawn	NJ	30000	201	555-1005
107	Anthony	William	900 Maple Road	Reading	MA	20000	617	555-1006
108	Poe	James	10 Preston Lane	Oakland	CA	40000	415	555-1007
109	Fiske	Robert	1500 Storybrook	Boston	MA	02098	617	555-1008
110	Porsena	Lars	110 Millbrook	Austin	TX	50000	512	555-1009
111	Alverez	Jose	25 Stuart Road	Miami	FL	60000	305	555-1010
112	Davis	John	26 Alpine Road	Elmherst	IL	50000	312	555-1020

A.

B.

C.

ID	LASTNAME	FIRST	STREET	CITY	ST	ZIP	AREA	PHONE
101	Culman	Tina	100 Elm Street	New Haven	CT	10000	203	555-1000
102	Benjamin	Nancy	25 Oak Street	Cambridge	MA	20000	617	555-1001
103	Kendall	Liz	14 Lark Ave.	Chicago	IL	20000	312	555-1002
104	Hogan	Dennis	40 Main Street	Edgewater	NJ	30000	201	555-1003
105	Swabey	Daphne	168 Bridge Road	Beverly	MA	20000	617	555-1004
106	Sobel	Carol	45 Porter Ave.	Fairlawn	NJ	30000	201	555-1005
107	Anthony	William	900 Maple Road	Reading	MA	20000	617	555-1006
109	Fiske	Robert	1500 Storybrook	Boston	MA	02098	617	555-1008
110	Porsena	Lars	110 Millbrook	Austin	TX	50000	512	555-1009
111	Alverez	Jose	25 Stuart Road	Miami	FL	60000	305	555-1010
112	Davis	John	26 Alpine Road	Elmherst	IL	50000	312	555-1020

A. The NAMELIST Database File

ID	DATE	AMOUNT
101	6/8/90	11.00
102	6/9/90	16.50
103	6/10/90	38.50
104	6/11/90	25.00
105	6/12/90	30.00
106	6/13/90	50.00
107	6/14/90	15.00
109	6/16/90	18.00
110	6/17/90	43.00
111	6/18/90	61.00
112	6/19/90	20.00

B. The AMOUNTS Database File

FIGURE 4   Linked Database Tables.   This database contains two tables. The first table (a) is used to store customer names, addresses, and phone numbers. The second table (b) is used to store any charges the customers make and the date they made them. When more than one table is used, they are linked using a common field that contains unique data, in this case, the customer's ID number.

FIGURE 5   Fields and Records.   A database is always organized into fields and records. Fields contain specific information about a person, item, or other subject. A group of fields makes up a record, a complete description of the person, item, or other subject.

Field

ID	LASTNAME	FIRST	STREET	CITY	ST	ZIP	AREA	PHONE
101	Culman	Tina	100 Elm Street	New Haven	CT	10000	203	555-1000
102	Benjamin	Nancy	25 Oak Street	Cambridge	MA	20000	617	555-1001
103	Kendall	Liz	14 Lark Ave.	Chicago	IL	20000	312	555-1002
104	Hogan	Dennis	40 Main Street	Edgewater	NJ	30000	201	555-1003
105	Swabey	Daphne	168 Bridge Road	Beverly	MA	20000	617	555-1004
106	Sobel	Carol	45 Porter Ave.	Fairlawn	NJ	30000	201	555-1005
107	Anthony	William	900 Maple Road	Reading	MA	20000	617	555-1006
108	Poe	James	10 Preston Lane	Oakland	CA	40000	415	555-1007
109	Fiske	Robert	1500 Storybrook	Boston	MA	02098	617	555-1008
110	Porsena	Lars	110 Millbrook	Austin	TX	50000	512	555-1009
111	Alverez	Jose	25 Stuart Road	Miami	FL	60000	305	555-1010
112	Davis	John	26 Alpine Road	Elmherst	IL	50000	312	555-1020

Record → (points to 104 Hogan record)

Step 2: Entering Data

Once you have defined the database file, you can enter data for each person. Database programs like dBASE display forms on the screen that display the field names you assigned. To enter data, you move the cursor from field to field and type in the data. The data you enter into the form is automatically entered into the database.

Step 3: Updating the Database

Whenever persons in your database move or change their names, their records must be updated to reflect the changes. To make these changes, the necessary files are opened, commands are used to locate the records, and the new data are entered in place of the old.

Step 4: Querying the Database

What if you want to call Liz Kendall, whose name and address have been entered into your database. To do so, you can query the database for all records where the last name is Kendall. When you execute the command, the record for any person whose last name is Kendall is displayed on the screen. If there is more than one Kendall, the first record for that name is displayed, and then you can scroll though all other records that have Kendall in them until you find the correct record. You can also link files so that you can query both at the same time.

Step 5: Printing Reports

One of the most valuable features of a database management program is its ability to generate reports. Reports are simply selected parts of the database displayed on the screen or printed out in a specified way. For example, using our database, you can print a report that lists just names, phone numbers, and amounts due or mailing labels that include complete addresses.

▼QUESTIONS

1. What is a database?
2. List three things you can do with the information stored in a database.
3. What is the difference between a record management program and a database management program?
4. What are two or three disadvantages of duplicating information when using a record management program?
5. What is the difference between physical storage and logical storage?
6. What is a database model? Which model is most frequently used for programs that run on microcomputers?
7. What are columns and rows called when discussed in the context of a relational database table?
8. What is the first step in creating a new database file? What do you do in this step?
9. What is a field? A record? Give examples of each.
10. What is it called when you change information in the database?
11. When do you query a database? What does a query do?
12. What is a printout of information in the database called?

TOPIC 1
Loading the Operating System

▼ CONCEPTS

To use a computer, you must first load the operating system. This is called booting the system. The term comes from the expression "pulling one's self up by the bootstraps." Once the operating system is loaded, you can load your applications programs or use the operating system's commands to manage your files.

▼ PROCEDURES

If your system is off, you can load the operating system by turning it on. When you do turn it on, it looks to the startup drive for the operating system files.

- On a floppy disk system, the startup drive is drive A, so you have to insert the DOS Startup disk into that drive. (See the box "Inserting Floppy Disks.")
- On a hard disk system, the startup drive is drive C. When you first turn on a hard disk system, be sure to open the door to drive A or eject the disk so that the program does not try to load the operating system from that drive.

▼ What Happens When You Boot a System

When you boot the computer, it always takes a few moments for the operating system to appear on the screen. During this pause, the computer is very busy.

1. The computer first executes a small program that is permanently stored in its read-only memory (ROM). This program instructs the computer to run diagnostic tests, which include checking the computer's memory to make certain it is operating correctly. If the computer finds a problem, it displays a message on the screen indicating where the problem is located and then stops.
2. If the diagnostics program finds no problems, the program in ROM executes two operating system programs on the disk in the startup drive (named IBMBIO.COM and IBMDOS.COM on IBM versions). If the disk does not have the two system files, the computer displays an error message and stops. If there is no disk in drive A and there is no hard disk, some systems automatically load BASIC, a programming language.

3. Once the two operating system programs are executed, the computer looks for a program called COMMAND.COM, which contains the most frequently used operating system commands. Executing this program loads a copy of it into RAM, where it remains as long as the computer has power.
4. The computer then looks for a configuration file named CONFIG.SYS. This file contains commands that customize the system.
5. The computer next looks for a batch file on the disk called AUTOEXEC.BAT. If this file is present, the computer executes whatever programs are listed there. If there is no AUTOEXEC.BAT file (and if the clock is not set automatically), the computer asks you to enter the date and time so that it can reset its internal clock. The process is now complete. The screen display depends on the operating system you are using and the contents of the AUTOEXEC.BAT file.

Inserting Floppy Disks

The way you insert a floppy disk depends on the type of system you are using. Most floppy disk systems have two drives, A and B. When loading a program, you insert the disk into drive A, the startup drive. To save your work onto a floppy disk, you insert it into drive B on a floppy disk computer and into drive A on a computer with a hard disk.

- To insert a $5\frac{1}{4}$-inch disk, open the door to the disk drive. Hold the disk with the label facing up to insert it into a horizontal drive. Hold it with the label facing to the left, and with the write-protect notch facing up, to insert it into a vertical drive. Point the oblong read/write slot toward the slot in the drive, and insert the disk into the slot. (On some systems, it clicks into place.) Never push hard because a $5\frac{1}{4}$-inch disk will buckle if it gets caught on an obstruction. Carefully jiggle the disk to make sure it is inserted all the way into the disk drive. Gently close the disk drive's door, or press the button that locks the disk into the drive. If you encounter any resistance, jiggle the disk, and then close the door or press the button again. To remove the disk, open the door and pull the disk out. On some drives, gently pushing it in and quickly releasing the pressure pops it out of the drive; on others, you have to press a button.

- To insert a $3\frac{1}{2}$-inch disk, hold it so that the arrow embossed on the case is facing up or to the left and pointing toward the drive's slot. Insert the disk gently into the drive, and then press until it clicks into place. To remove the disk, press the disk eject button above or below the drive's slot.

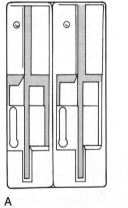
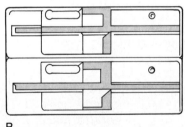

A   B

A. If your floppy disks are side by side, drive A is the one on the left.
B. If one drive is above the other, drive A is the one on the top.

With the drives set, you turn on the computer. This is called a cold boot and is the method you use when you begin a session with your computer. (See the tip on warm booting the computer in the "TIPS" section.) If your system is not equipped with a clock, you are prompted to enter the date and time when you boot it. If you are prompted to do so, or if you want to change the date or time, see the box "Entering or Changing Dates and Times."

If you are already running an applications program, you do not have to boot the system to return to DOS since it is already in memory. You just use the applications program's Quit or Exit command, and that returns you to the operating system.

Entering or Changing Dates and Times

When you first turn on some systems, you are prompted to enter the date and time. At other times, you can change the date and time for a session using the DATE and TIME commands from the command prompt or the *Set Date and Time* choice on the DOS 4 Shell's DOS Utilities' subgroup. Entering the correct date and time into your system's clock is important because the clock date and time marks files that you save. These are helpful if you have several files containing the same data and you forget which is the most recent version. The clock is also used by many applications programs to enter the date and time into files that you create.

You enter the date and time as described below. If you enter either incorrectly, an error message is displayed, and you are prompted to reenter them.

ENTERING DATES
Enter dates in the format MM-DD-YY.

- MM is a number from 1 to 12.
- DD is a number from 1 to 31.
- YY is a number from 80 to 99.

You can use dashes (-), slashes (/), or periods (.) to separate the day, month, and year. For example, to enter the date January 10, 1992, enter it as 1-10-92, 1/10/92, or 1.10.92. You cannot enter a date earlier than 1/1/1980. To enter a date later than 12/31/1999, you must enter all four digits for the year. For example, to enter January 1, 2001, type **1/1/2001**. If you fail to enter a date, the system's clock remains set to 1-01-80, and all files that you save are marked with that date.

ENTERING TIMES
Enter times in the format Hours:Minutes:Seconds:100ths seconds. (Seconds and 100ths seconds are optional and rarely used by most users, and some systems do not accept 100ths.)

- Hours is a number between 0 and 23.
- Minutes is a number between 0 and 59.
- Seconds is a number between 0 and 59.
- 100ths seconds is a number between 0 and 99.

You separate the hours, minutes, and seconds with colons (:) or periods (.). You separate the seconds and hundredths of seconds with a period or comma. You can use 24-hour military time on DOS 3 and 4 or 12-hour standard time if you are using DOS 4.

- Military time is based on a 24-hour day. For example, to set the clock to 1:30pm, enter **13:30**.
- Standard time is based on a 12-hour period. To specify the time when using DOS 4, you must enter a **p** or **a** after the last time unit. For example, to set the clock to 1:30pm, enter **1:30p**. To set it to 10:30am, enter **10:30a**. Do not use spaces between the time and the letters.

 Error Messages

When you boot an IBM computer system, you may see the error message *Non-System disk or disk error* (or a similar one on compatible computers). This appears when you turn on the computer with a disk in drive A that does not contain the operating system files that the computer needs. If you get this message, insert the DOS disk into drive A or open the drive's door if it is a hard disk system, and then reboot.

THE COMMAND PROMPT AND THE DOS 4 SHELL

When you load DOS, either the command prompt or the DOS 4 Shell is displayed. Which appears depends on the version of DOS that you are using and how your system has been set up.

The Command Prompt

On some systems, the command prompt appears on the screen when you boot the system (Figure 6). It will normally be *A>* or *A:\>* if you loaded from a floppy disk or *C:\>* if you loaded from a hard disk drive. However, the command prompt can be customized, so it may be different on your system.

The command prompt tells you that you are in DOS and that the default, or active, disk drive is drive A or C (see Appendix). From this command prompt, you can execute all DOS commands or start applications programs like WordPerfect®, Lotus® 1-2-3®, or dBASE®.

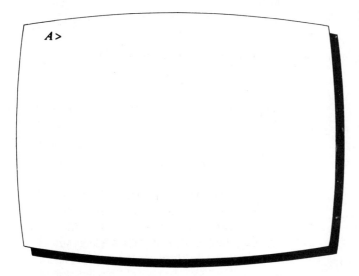

FIGURE 6   The Command Prompt. When you load DOS without loading the Shell, the screen displays the command prompt.

The DOS 4 Shell

If you are using DOS 4, and your system has been set up to do so, the DOS 4 Shell appears on the screen when you boot the system. The first screen displayed is the Start Programs screen (Figure 7). The menu-operated Shell makes it easy to execute commands without remembering cryptic commands. All you have to know is how to use the Shell's menus.

Although you might want to use the Shell for most of your work, some advanced procedures can be completed only from the command prompt. You can quickly switch back and forth between the Shell and the command prompt whenever you want to. When the command prompt is displayed, the system works just like earlier versions of DOS.

- To display the Shell from the command prompt, type **DOSSHELL** and then press ENTER.
  - If you are working on a hard disk system, you must first type **C:** and then press ENTER.
  - If you are working on a floppy disk system, you must first insert the Shell disk into drive A, type **A:** and then press ENTER.

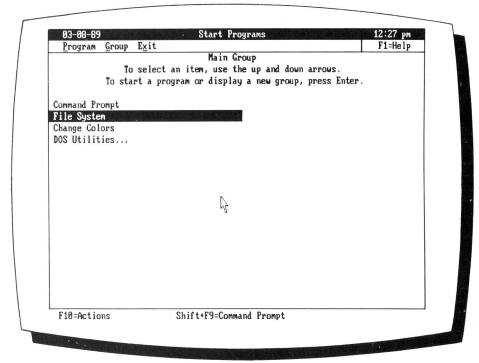

```
┌─────────────────────────────────────────────────────┐
│ 03-08-89             Start Programs        12:27 pm   │
│ Program  Group  Exit                       │ F1=Help  │
│                     Main Group                        │
│         To select an item, use the up and down arrows.│
│       To start a program or display a new group, press Enter.│
│                                                       │
│ Command Prompt                                        │
│ File System                                           │
│ Change Colors                                         │
│ DOS Utilities...                                      │
│                                                       │
│                                                       │
│                                                       │
│                          ⇖                            │
│                                                       │
│                                                       │
│                                                       │
│                                                       │
│                                                       │
│  F10=Actions            Shift+F9=Command Prompt       │
└─────────────────────────────────────────────────────┘
```

FIGURE 7   The DOS 4 Shell Start Programs Screen.   The Start Programs screen is the first screen displayed when you load the Shell.

- To display the command prompt when the Shell is on the screen, you have two choices:
  - Press F3 from Start Programs to remove the Shell from memory. (You first have to press F3 if you are in the File System, or ESC if you are in the DOS Utilities' subgroup, to return to Start Programs.) You can also select *Exit Shell* from the Start Programs' Exit menu on the Action Bar. After using either command, type **DOSSHELL** and then press ENTER to return to the Shell.
  - Press SHIFT-F9 to leave the Shell in memory and load a second copy of the COMMAND.COM file. You can also select *Command Prompt* from the Start Programs' Main Group. These commands make it faster to return to the Shell when you want. To do so, type **EXIT** and then press ENTER. If you use this command, and there is not enough room in memory for the second copy of the COMMAND.COM program, an error message is displayed. Use the first procedure to display the command prompt.

QUITTING DOS

When you are done for the day, you should always turn off the computer. Before doing so, open the drive doors or eject your disks and remove them. Then, turn off the computer and the display using the same switches you used to turn them on.

If you are using the DOS 4 Shell, you should always press F3 to exit the Shell and return to the command prompt before turning off your system. If your operating system is set up with a startup option named SWAP, turning the computer off without first exiting the Shell leaves temporary files on your disk. If you do this repeatedly, you will eventually run out of room on the disk.

11

▼TIPS

➤ **You can also warm boot a computer.** This means the computer is already on. To warm boot the system, you hold down CTRL and ALT while pressing DEL or press the computer's reset button. This command clears all data from the computer's memory and has almost the same effect as turning the computer off and then back on again. Use this command (and the reset button and on/off switch) with caution. You normally use this procedure only when you encounter a problem with your system. You should not warm boot regularly. It doesn't cause harm, but it is a bad habit because you might lose data if you do it at the wrong time.

➤ **If you turn on some floppy disk systems without a disk in drive A, the Basic program is loaded from ROM.** If this happens (the screen indicates that you are in the Basic program), insert the DOS disk, type **SYSTEM** and then press ENTER to display the command prompt.

➤ **To load the DOS 4 Shell from the command prompt, or return to it after completing commands,** you must first insert the Shell disk into drive A if you are using a floppy disk system.
  - If you see the message *Insert diskette with \COMMAND.COM in drive x and press any key when ready* (the *x* is the specified drive and varies depending on the system you are using), it means you should insert the Startup disk into the requested drive and then press any key to continue.
  - If you see the message *Insert disk with batch file* on a floppy disk system, it usually means you should reinsert the Shell disk and then press any key to continue.

➤ **After loading DOS, you can check the version number whenever the command prompt is displayed.** To do so, type **VER** and then press ENTER. This is useful when you have more than one version of DOS and cannot remember which one you loaded into memory. Since the programs used by some DOS commands are stored on a disk until you need them, you should always insert the operating system disk with the same version of DOS as the one in memory. If you use the wrong version, you will get an error message. You can first use the VER command to find out which version is in memory, and then insert the correct disk when using external commands.

➤ **When you turn your computer off,** you should wait 20 to 30 seconds before turning it back on. Some systems will not reboot without this pause. If you turn one of these systems back on too quickly, nothing happens.

NOTE ON TUTORIALS

The way you load the operating system depends on whether you are loading DOS 3 or 4. For this reason, there are two tutorials in this topic, but you only complete the one for the version of the operating system that you are using.

- Tutorial 1A describes loading and quitting DOS 3.
- Tutorial 1B describes loading and quitting DOS 4.

Also, if the computer that you are working on is connected to a network, you may have special procedures to follow to access the operating system. If so, your instructor will provide you with information on how to begin.

TUTORIAL 1A
Loading and Quitting DOS 3

In this tutorial, you load DOS 3 and then quit it. To begin this tutorial, your computer should be off.

Step 1 **Get Ready.** If you are working on a floppy disk system, insert the DOS disk into drive A (see the box "Inserting Floppy Disks"). If you are working on a hard disk system, open the door to drive A or eject the disk in that drive.

Step 2 **Load the Operating System.** To load the operating system, turn on the computer. The On/Off switch is usually located on the side of the computer toward the rear. When you turn the computer on, a bright underline flashes in the upper left corner of the screen as the computer runs its internal diagnostic program. In a few moments, the computer may beep, and then drive A spins and its light comes on while the operating system is loaded. If there is no disk in drive A, the computer looks to drive C for the program if the system contains a hard disk drive. If nothing appears on your screen, your display may not be on. On some systems, the display has a separate On/Off switch.

Step 3 **Enter the Date and Time.** If your computer does not have a clock that is set automatically, in a moment the prompt reads *Enter new date:*. (If you make a typo when entering any commands, press BACKSPACE to delete the incorrect characters, and then type them in correctly before pressing ENTER.)

1. Enter the date as month-day-year (for example, type **01-30-90** for January 30, 1990), and then press ENTER. The prompt then reads *Enter new time:*.
2. Enter the time as hour:minute (for example, type **1:30**), and then press ENTER.

Result. The command prompt appears on the screen.

Step 4 **Check the Version Number.** After loading DOS, you can check the version number whenever the command prompt is displayed.

Note. In all the instructions in this text, the characters you type are shown in uppercase letters, but whether you use uppercase or lowercase letters usually does not matter. For example, in the following command, you can type **VER**, **ver**, **Ver**, **vEr**, or **veR**, and the computer accepts them all.

To check the version number
    Type   **VER** and then press ENTER

Result. The screen displays the version number of the DOS in memory.

Step 5 **Continue or Quit.** You have now completed this tutorial. Either continue to the next tutorial or quit for the day. If you want to quit, remove your disks from the drives and turn off the computer.

13

TUTORIAL 1B
Loading and Quitting DOS 4

In this tutorial, you load DOS 4 and then quit it. To begin this tutorial, your computer should be off.

Step 1   **Get Ready.** If you are working on a floppy disk system, insert the Startup disk into drive A (see the box ''Inserting Floppy Disks''). If you are working on a hard disk system, open the door to drive A or eject the disk in that drive.

Step 2   **Load the Operating System.** To load the operating system, turn on the computer. The On/Off switch is usually located on the side of the computer toward the rear. When you turn the computer on, a bright underline flashes in the upper left corner of the screen as the computer runs its internal diagnostic program. In a few moments, the computer may beep, and then drive A spins and its light comes on while the operating system is loaded. If there is no disk in drive A, the computer looks to drive C for the program if the system contains a hard disk drive. If nothing appears on your screen, your display may not be on. On some systems, the display has a separate On/Off switch.

Step 3   **Enter the Date and Time.** If your computer does not have a clock that is set automatically, in a moment, the prompt reads *Enter new date:*. (If you make a typo when entering any commands, press BACKSPACE to delete the incorrect characters, and then type them in correctly before pressing ENTER.)

      1. Enter the date as month-day-year (for example, type **01-30-90** for January 30, 1990), and then press ENTER. The prompt then reads *Enter new time:*.
      2. Enter the time as hour:minute (for example, type **1:30** and add an **a** or a **p** to specify A.M. or P.M.), and then press ENTER.

Result.   The command prompt *A:\>* or *C:\>* appears on the screen, or the DOS 4 Shell is displayed. If the command prompt is displayed and you are working on a floppy disk system, insert the Shell disk into drive A. (On a hard disk system, this isn't necessary.) Type **DOSSHELL** and then press ENTER.

Step 4   **Return to the Command Prompt.** Whenever the Shell is displayed, you can remove it from memory and return to the command prompt.

To return to the command prompt
      Press   F3

Result.   The command prompt appears on the screen.

Step 5   **Check the Version Number.** After loading DOS, you can check the version number whenever the command prompt is displayed.

Note.   In all the instructions in this text, the characters you type are shown in uppercase letters, but whether you use uppercase or lowercase letters usually does not matter. For example, in the following command, you can type **VER**, **ver**, **Ver**, **vEr**, or **veR**, and the computer accepts them all.

To check the version number
      Type   **VER** and then press ENTER

Result.   The screen displays the version number of the DOS in memory.

Step 6   **Return to the Shell.** Now, return to the Shell.

To load the Shell
      Type   **DOSSHELL** and then press ENTER

Result.   The Shell reappears on the screen.

Step 7   **Load a Second Copy of DOS.** Instead of exiting the Shell, you can display the command prompt by running a second copy of the COMMAND.COM file.

To load a second copy of DOS
   Press   SHIFT-F9

Result.   The command prompt appears on the screen, and a message at the top of the screen reads *When ready to return to the DOS Shell, type EXIT then press enter.* If your system does not have enough memory for a second copy of DOS, an error message is displayed. Follow the instructions that appear on the screen to cancel the command, and then proceed to Step 9.

Step 8   **Return to the Shell.** Now, return to the Shell by removing the second copy of COMMAND.COM from memory.

To return to the Shell
   Type   **EXIT** and then press ENTER

Result.   The Shell reappears on the screen.

Step 9   **Continue or Quit.** You have now completed this tutorial. Either continue to the next tutorial or quit for the day.

To return to the command prompt
   Press   F3 to return to the command prompt

Result.   If you want to quit, remove your disks from the drives and turn off the computer.

▼ EXERCISES

EXERCISE 1A   Booting Your System

The way you boot a system varies, depending on how your system has been set up. If your system is on a network, or for some other reason your startup does not follow the same rules described in this topic, enter your startup procedures here.

1. _____
   _____
   _____
2. _____
   _____
   _____
3. _____
   _____
   _____
4. _____
   _____
   _____

EXERCISE 1B   View a Video

Many videocassettes have been developed to introduce users to specific operating systems. Visit your library, learning center, and computer lab to see if any are available for you to view. If so, view it, and then summarize its key points.

15

▼QUESTIONS

1. What does booting a computer mean?
2. What is the startup drive? Which drive is it on a floppy disk system? On a hard disk system?
3. What is the difference between a warm boot and a cold boot? How do you do each?
4. When running DOS 4, what is the difference between removing the Shell from memory and running a second copy of COMMAND.COM?
5. Why should you remove the DOS 4 Shell from memory before you turn off your computer?
6. Why would you want to use the VER command to find out which version of DOS is in your computer's memory?

TOPIC 2
Loading dBASE

▼ CONCEPTS

Before you can load dBASE, you must load the computer's operating system. Once the operating system is loaded, the way you then load dBASE depends on the type of computer you are using and the operating system you loaded. (Note that dBASE IV runs only on a hard disk system.)

▼ PROCEDURES

This section describes the procedures that you follow to:

- Load dBASE IV from the system prompt
- Load dBASE IV from the DOS 4 Shell

To Load dBASE from the System Prompt

When the system prompt is displayed on the screen:

1. Change the default drive and directory to the one containing the DBASE.EXE file.
   - If the system prompt is not *C>* or *C:\>*, type **c:** and then press ENTER to change the drive.
   - To change the default directory, type **cd** then type the name of the directory, and then press ENTER. For example, if the program files are in a directory named DBASE, type **cd\DBASE** and then press ENTER.
2. Type **DBASE** and then press ENTER to load the program. The drive spins, and the license agreement screen appears. Press ENTER to display the dBASE IV Control Center screen (Figure 8). (When the license agreement appears, you can also wait a moment instead of pressing ENTER to display the Control Center.)

To Load dBASE from the DOS 4 Shell

When the DOS 4 Shell is displayed on the screen:

1. To display the File System, highlight *File System* on the Start Programs' Main Group, and then press ENTER. All the files on the disk in the default drive are automatically listed.
2. To specify the drive, press TAB to move the highlight to the Drive Identifier area, highlight the drive that contains the dBASE IV program files, and then press ENTER.
3. To specify the directory, press TAB to move the highlight to the Directory Tree area, highlight the directory that contains the dBASE IV files, and then pressure ENTER to make it the default directory and list the files it contains.
4. To load the program, press TAB to move the highlight to the File List, highlight the program file named *DBASE.EXE,* and then press SPACEBAR to select the file. Press F10 to activate the Action Bar, press F for *File* to pull down the File menu, and then press O for *open (start)* to display a pop-up with the cursor in the *Options* entry field. Press ENTER without specifying any options. The drive spins, and the licence agreement screen appears. Press ENTER to display the dBASE IV Control Center screen (Figure 8).

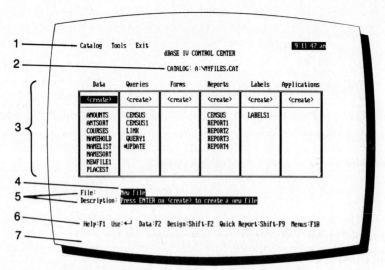

FIGURE 8   The dBASE IV Control Center.   The dBASE IV Control Center screen display has the following elements:
1. A menu bar contains pull down menus (see Figure 9 on page 24)
2. The current catalog line identifies the catalog that is currently open
3. Work surface contains six panels that list all files in the catalog
4. The highlight is moved around the work surface to select files listed in the panels
5. The current file and description line identifies the highlighted file
6. The navigation line lists the keys that you can press
7. The message line displays prompts and messages

(When the license agreement appears, you can also wait a moment instead of pressing ENTER to display the Control Center.)

THE CONTROL CENTER

When you load dBASE IV, the Control Center is displayed on the screen (Figure 8). This screen organizes all the files you work on. You will learn more about the items on this screen as you proceed through this part, but here is a brief description of each:

1. The menu bar contains menus that are displayed when you press F10. You will see how to use these menus in Topic 3. The current time is displayed at the right end of this line.
2. The current catalog line lists the catalog that is currently in memory. A catalog contains related files so that they are easy for you to access. The current catalog listing is simply the name of the catalog in use preceded by its path. For example, C:\UNTITLED.CAT indicates that the current catalog is named UNTITLED.CAT on drive C.
3. The work surface is divided into six panels that list the contents of the current catalog. These contents are actually files that are listed as you create them.
4. The current file and description section identifies the object that is currently highlighted in one of the work surface panels.
5. The navigation line lists the keys that you can press to perform actions. The keys listed on this line depend on where you are in the system.
6. The message line displays messages and prompts. For example, when the highlight is on a menu choice, a description of that choice is displayed on this line.

CLEARING OR QUITTING

When you work on dBASE IV, the program opens files that you must close before quitting the program or working on another project. If you turn off or reboot the computer without quitting properly, files you have been working on may be damaged, and data may be lost. When the Control Center is displayed, you use one of the menu choices to close the open files and return to the operating system.

To Quit dBASE IV

1. Press F10 to activate the menus.
2. Press → (if necessary) to highlight *Exit.*
3. Press ↓ to highlight the command *Quit to DOS,* and then press ENTER. The message *** *END RUN dBASE IV* is displayed, and the operating system reappears.

TIP

➤ **You can use a shortcut to quit the program when the Control Center is displayed.** Press ALT-E to pull down the Exit menu, and then press Q for *Quit to DOS.*

19

TUTORIAL 2A
Loading dBASE from the Command Prompt

In this tutorial, you load and then exit dBASE from the system prompt. To begin this tutorial, the computer must be off.

Step 1   **Load dBASE.** Before you can use the dBASE program, you must load it into your computer's memory.

- Turn the computer on. (If a prompt on the screen asks you to enter the date and time, see the box ''Entering or Changing Dates and Times'' in Topic 1.) In a moment, the system prompt *C>* or *C:\>* is displayed. If the DOS 4 Shell is displayed, press F3 to return to the system prompt.
- Type **CD\DBASE** (or substitute your own directory name if the files are not stored in a directory named DBASE) to change to the directory that contains the dBASE IV program files.
- Type **DBASE** and then press ENTER.

Result.   The drive spins, and the license agreement screen appears. Press ENTER to display the Control Center (Figure 8).

Step 2   **Continue or Quit.** You have now completed this tutorial. Either continue with the next tutorial or exist dBASE and return to the operating system.

To quit dBASE and return to the operating system

Press   F10 to activate the menu
Press   → (if necessary) to highlight *Exit* and pull down the menu
Press   Q for *Quit to DOS*, and then press ENTER

Result.   The message *** *END RUN dBASE IV* is displayed, and the command prompt reappears. Remove your program and data disks, and then turn off the computer or load another program.

TUTORIAL 2B
Loading dBASE from the DOS 4 Shell

In this tutorial, you load and then exit dBASE from the Shell. You can complete this tutorial only if you are using DOS 4 or later versions. To begin this tutorial, the Shell must be displayed (see Topic 1).

Step 1   **Display the File System.** The command you use to load programs is contained in the File System.

To display the File System

Highlight   *File System,* and then press ENTER

Result.   The File System screen is displayed. All the files on the disk in drive C are automatically listed.

Step 2   **Change the Default Directory.** Change to the directory that contains the dBASE IV program files.

To change directories

Press   TAB to move the highlight to the Directory Tree
Highlight   *DBASE* (or your own directory name if the files are not stored in a directory named DBASE), and then press ENTER

Result. A list of the files in the DBASE directory is displayed.

Step 3 **Load dBASE.** To load dBASE, you select the program's name on the File List, and then select *Open (start)* from the File menu.

To load dBASE

Press   TAB to move the highlight to the File List
Highlight   the file named DBASE.EXE
Press   SPACEBAR to select the file
Press   F10 to activate the Action Bar
Press   F for *File* to pull down the File menu
Press   O for *Open (start)* to display a pop-up with the cursor in the *Options* entry field
Press   ENTER without specifying any options

Result. The drive spins, and the license agreement screen appears. Press ENTER to display the Control Center (Figure 8).

Step 4 **Quit dBASE.** When you are finished working with dBASE, you must quit the program correctly, or you may lose data.

To quit dBASE and return to the operating system

Press   F10 to activate the menu
Press   → (if necessary) to highlight *Exit* and pull down the menu
Press   Q for *Quit to Dos*, and then press ENTER

Result. The message *** *END RUN dBASE IV* is displayed and the File System reappears.

Step 5 **Continue or Quit.** You have now completed this tutorial. Either continue with the next tutorial or return to the command prompt and quit the program.

To quit the program

Press   F3 to return to the Start Programs screen
Press   F3 to return to the system prompt

Result. The command prompt is displayed. Remove your disks from the drives, put them in their envelopes, and then turn off the computer.

▼**EXERCISE**

EXERCISE 2A   Identify the Items on the Screen

After loading dBASE so the Control Center is displayed, turn your printer on. Press SHIFT-PRTSC (or just PRINT SCREEN on an enhanced keyboard) to make a printout of the screen display, and then advance the paper out of the printer. Using Figure 8 as a guide, identify the items that appear on the screen by circling them and writing a brief description of what they indicate. Graphics characters, like those used in borders, may not print or may print as other characters. If this happens, draw them on your printout or ignore them.

21

QUESTIONS

1. List the steps you would follow to load dBASE from the command prompt. From the DOS 4 Shell.
2. List the names of the parts of the Control Center, and briefly describe each.
3. Why should you correctly quit the dBASE program?

▼CONCEPTS

When you load dBASE IV, it displays the Control Center. This screen links you to the database files that you create and the other files that you create to work with your databases. You execute commands from this screen using menus or the work surface. As you do so, on-line help is available at any time.

All screens have work surfaces in addition to menus. You use these work surfaces to enter, view, or lay out databases and associated files. These work surfaces vary, depending on the activity you are performing at the moment. For example, the Control Center's work surface contains six panels. When you create or retrieve a catalog, all the files in the catalog are listed in one of the panels described in Table 1. As you create new files for the current catalog, they are also listed in one of the panels.

Each work surface contains a cursor (also called a highlight) that you use to point to items on the surface. The cursor changes shape depending on what screen is displayed. Sometimes the cursor is only an underscore character; other times it is a bar. To move the cursor, you press the navigation keys that work on the current surface. These keys vary, depending on the surface you are working on, but always include the arrow keys, TAB, and BACKTAB.

TABLE 1   The Control Center's Work Surface Panels

Panel	Description
Data	Creates and lists databases used to store data (see Topic 4)
Queries	Creates and lists queries that allow you to work with just selected parts of your database files (see Topic 10) or link files (see Topic 14)
Forms	Creates layouts that display your data in a customized format
Reports	Creates and lists formats for printed reports to make the data more useful and attractive (see Topic 13)
Labels	Creates and lists formats for printed labels that you can use for mailings, file folders, and disks (see Topic 12)
Applications	Creates and lists programs that group commands together so that they are performed automatically when you run the file in which they are stored

▼PROCEDURES

This section describes the procedures that you follow to:

- Use menus
- Open and close files from the Control Center
- Use function keys
- Display on-line help
- Cancel a command

USING MENUS

Many commands are listed on pull-down menus (Figure 9). There are two ways to pull down these menus so that you can make choices:

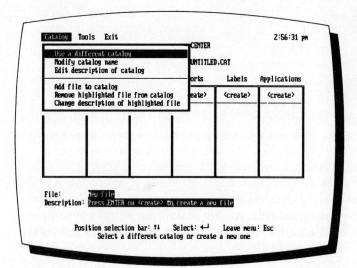

FIGURE 9 The Control Center's Menus. You press F10 to activate the pull-down menus. You then use the arrow keys to pull down other menus or highlight choices listed on the menus. Pressing ENTER executes the highlighted menu choice.

TABLE 2   Menu Commands

To	Press
Commands That Pull Down Menus	
Pull down a menu	F10
Pull down a specific menu	ALT-FIRST letter
Pull down other menus	→ or ←
Commands That Make Choices from a	
Pulled-down Menu	
Highlight menu choices	↓ or ↑
Highlight the last choice on a meau	PGDN or END
Highlight the first choice on a menu	PGUP or HOME
Select the highlighted menu choice	ENTER
Highlight and select a menu choice	First letter in choice's name
Back up through menus or return to the Control Center	ESC

- Press F10. This pulls down the first menu if you have not previously made menu choices. If you have the last menu that you used is pulled down.
- Hold down ALT and press the first letter in any menu name to pull down that specific menu; for example, to pull down the Exit menu, press ALT-E.

Once a menu is pulled down, you can exit the menus, pull down additional menus, or make choices (see Table 2).

- Press ESC to leave the menus without making a choice.
- To pull down another menu, press → or ← to highlight its name on the menu bar. Alternatively, hold down ALT and press the first letter in the menu's name.
- When a menu is pulled down, there are two ways that you can select one of the listed commands.
  - Press ↓ or ↑ to move the highlight between choices, or press HOME or END to move the cursor to the first and last choices. As you do so, the message line below the navigation line displays a brief description of the highlighted choice. When you have highlighted the desired choice, press ENTER.
  - Press the first letter in the menu choice's name to execute it.

As you work with menus, you will encounter shaded menu choices and choices preceded by an arrowhead (▶) character.

- A shaded choice appears darker than the other choices on the menu. (Adjust your display's contrast or brightness control if this difference isn't obvious.) This shading indicates that the command is not available at the current point in the procedure.
- An arrowhead (▶) character indicates that choosing the command displays a submenu.

OPENING AND CLOSING FILES

To work with files, you have to first open the file by selecting it. When you are finished with the file, you then close it. When you select a file, its name moves to the top of the panel and is separated from other, unselected files with a thin ruled line.

Opening Files

To select a file listed in one of the panels on the Control Center's work surface, you first press the left and right arrow keys, or press TAB and BACKTAB to move the highlight to the appropriate panel. You highlight the file's name, and then press ENTER. This displays a prompt box offering choices such as *Use File*. To select one of these choices, highlight it, and then press ENTER. You can avoid the prompt box by highlighting the file's name and then quickly pressing ENTER twice.

There are also shortcuts to selecting files. For example, you can highlight a file's name, and then press F2 to display its data or SHIFT-F2 to display its design. You'll learn more about these shortcuts as you complete the tutorials in this part.

 Error Messages

If you enter any commands incorrectly, an error box is displayed. These boxes describe the problem, and offer you three choices. You can select one of them either by pressing the first letter in its name or by highlighting it and then pressing ENTER.

- *Cancel* cancels the command.
- *Edit* allows you to reenter the command.
- *Help* displays help on the problem.

 The Optional Dot Prompt

When dBASE was first introduced, all commands were executed by typing them from the dot prompt, which was simply a period displayed on the screen. This method of executing commands has been retained in dBASE IV but is only for advanced users. (When the dot prompt is displayed, the status bar at the bottom of the screen displays *Command*.) If you select a menu choice that returns you to this dot prompt you have two choices (other than entering commands to manipulate the database).

- Press F2 to return to the Control Center, or
- Type QUIT and then press ENTER to quit dBASE and return to the operating system.

When you first begin to use dBASE, no files have been created. The only object listed in each panel is the ⟨*create*⟩ choice. You use this choice to create files. For example, to create a new database file, you press the arrow keys or TAB to move the highlight to the Data panel, highlight ⟨*create*⟩, and then press ENTER.

Closing Files

To close a file (move it back below the horizontal line), highlight its name in the Control Center's panel, and then press ENTER. This displays a prompt box offering choices such as *Close File*. To select one of these choices, highlight it, and then press ENTER. You can avoid the prompt box by highlighting the file's name and then quickly pressing ENTER twice.

FUNCTION KEYS

Many of the most frequently used commands are assigned to function keys. To execute one of these commands, you press the appropriate function key, either by itself or while holding down SHIFT. To help you remember the tasks assigned to these keys, the program has a keyboard template that lists each key and its function (Figure 10). Table 3 describes the keys and the tasks they perform.

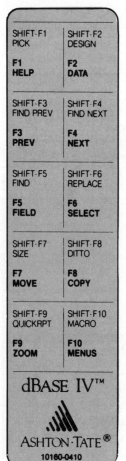

FIGURE 10 Keyboard Template. The keyboard template lists the functions assigned to each of the function keys.

TABLE 3 Function Keys

Key	Name	Task
F1	Help	Displays help
F2	Data	Displays data in Browse or Edit mode
F3	Previous	• In Browse or Edit mode, moves the highlight to the previous field. In Edit mode, if you press it with the highlight in the first field, the previous record is displayed. • In help, displays the previous page • In Queries, moves the highlight to the next object
F4	Next	• In Browse or Edit mode, moves the highlight to the next field. In Edit mode, if you press it with the highlight in the last field, the next record is displayed. • In help, displays the next page • In Queries, moves the highlight to the next object
F5	Field	• On a layout surface, adds or modifies a field • On the view skeleton, adds or removes a field
F6	Extend select	Selects adjacent text and fields
F7	Move	Moves selected text and fields
F8	Copy	Copies selected text or fields
F9	Zoom	Expands or shrinks memo fields, condition boxes, some data fill-in fields, and file skeletons
F10	Menu	Pulls down the menus
Shift-F1	Pick	Displays a list of items available for current fill in
Shift-F2	Design	Displays design screens
Shift-F3	Find previous	Moves the highlight to the previous occurrence of a search string
Shift-F4	Find next	Moves the highlight to the next occurrence of a search string
Shift-F5	Find	Finds a specified search string
Shift-F6	Replace	Replaces a search string with another string
Shift-F7	Size	Changes the size of design elements; in Browse mode, it changes the width of columns
Shift-F8	Ditto	Copies data from the same field in the previous record in the current field
Shift-F9	Quick report	Prints a quick report of the data
Shift-F10	Macro	Displays a macros prompt box

ON-LINE HELP

dBASE IV provides extensive on-line help, which you can display at any time by pressing F1 (Figure 11). When you do so, a help box appears. Help is context sensitive; that is, the help that is displayed depends on where the highlight is when you press F1. The help box contains four parts:

1. The title line identifies the topic of the help currently displayed.
2. The text area displays the actual help text that you read to learn about procedures. If the help text on the current topic is too long to be displayed on one screen, the message ⟨*MORE F4*⟩ is displayed in the lower right-hand corner of the text area. Press F4 to continue reading.
3. Buttons allow you to move to other help topics. To select one of them:

27

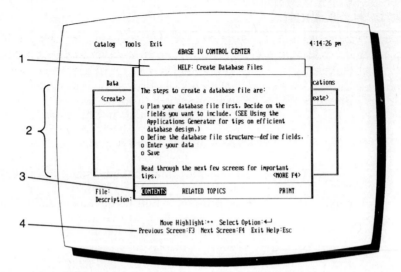

FIGURE 11   On-Line Help.   When you press **F1** to display help, a help box containing four parts is displayed.
1. The Title Line
2. The Text Area
3. Buttons
4. Contents Navigation Line

- Press the left or right arrow keys, SPACEBAR, or BACKSPACE to highlight its name, and then press ENTER.
- Press the first letter in its name.
4. The contents navigation line lists keys that you can press to navigate the help system.

When a help box is displayed, you can display additional help topics by pressing any of the keys described in Table 4. You can also use the arrow keys to move the highlight over any of the buttons listed in the help box and described in Table 5, and then press ENTER. To exit help and return to where you were, press ESC. You may have to press it more than once, depending on where you are in the help system.

TABLE 4   Help Keys

To	Press
Display next screen, if any	F4
Display previous screen, if any	F3
Exit help	ESC

TABLE 5   Help Buttons

Button	Description
CONTENTS	Displays a table of contents for all help topics. You use the up and down arrow keys to highlight any topic, and then press ENTER for help on that topic. You can also press F3 to display more general help or F4 to display more specific help.
RELATED TOPICS	Displays an index of related topics. You use the up and down arrows keys to highlight any topic, and then press ENTER for help on that topic.
BACKUP	Displays the previous screen if there is one.
PRINT	Prints the currently displayed help screen.

CANCELING A COMMAND

When you are in the middle of a procedure, you can press Esc to cancel it. When you do so, the prompt reads *Are you sure you want to abandon operation?* Press Y to return to the Control Center, or press N to continue without canceling the command.

TUTORIAL 3A
Getting Acquainted with dBASE IV

In this tutorial, you explore help and operate the menus. To begin this tutorial, you must first load the program (see Topic 2).

Step 1   **Explore Help.** You can get help on the program while using dBASE by just pressing F1. This displays the help box from which you can select topics you want help on.

To display help

Press   F1 to display the help box

Result.   The help box is displayed (Figure 11). To display additional help, press F4. To back up to the previous help screen, press F3. When you are finished, press Esc to return to the Control Center.

Step 2   **Use the Help Options.** You can get help by using the options displayed in the help menu.

To display help on a specific command

Press   F1 to display the help box
Highlight   *CONTENTS* button, and then press ENTER
Highlight   *About Database Files,* and then press ENTER
Press   F4 to display additional help
Highlight   *RELATED TOPICS* button, and then press ENTER
Highlight   *Help on Help*, and then press ENTER

Result.   The *Help on Help* choice is displayed. Press F4 to display additional help. If you want to print this help, be sure the print is on. Highlight the *PRINT* button, and then press ENTER. When you are finished, press Esc to return to the Control Center.

Step 3   **Explore Menus.** Now, let's explore the pull-down menus.

To explore menus

Press   F10 to pull down a menu
Press   → repeatedly to pull down other menus

Result.   As you press the arrow keys, the menus are pulled down one after another.

Step 4   **Execute Commands.** Let's now execute a command that sets the program so that instructions are provided as you execute commands.

To execute a command

Press   ALT-T to pull down the Tools menu
Press   END to highlight *Settings*, the last menu choice
Press   ENTER to select *Settings*
Press   ↓ to move the highlight over *Instruct*

Result.   The menu choice *Instruct* is followed by the current setting—either *ON* or *OFF*. Press ENTER a few times, and the setting changes each time you press it. Be sure the setting is set to *ON*, and then press Esc to leave the menu and return to the Control Center.

Step 5   **Continue or Quit.** You have now completed this tutorial. Either continue with the next tutorial or quit the program.

▼EXERCISES

EXERCISE 3A   Explore Menus

Turn your printer on, and then pull down the Tools menu and select *Settings*. Press SHIFT-PRTSC (or just PRINT SCREEN on an enhanced keyboard) to make a printout of the menu. On the printout, list the steps that you took to pull down the menu.

EXERCISE 3B   Explore Help

Turn your printer on, and then explore the help system. When you find a topic of interest, make a printout using the *PRINT* button displayed on the bottom line of the help box.

▼QUESTIONS

1. What key do you press to activate the menu bar? What keys do you press to pull down a specific menu?
2. When the menu bar is activated, what keys can you press to pull down other menus? To make choices from the menu?
3. How do you open and close files displayed on the Control Center?
4. What key do you press to display help? What is a button?
5. What does it mean when you say help is context sensitive?

▼CONCEPTS

The first step in using a database management program is to define the database file you want to store data in. To define a database, you must know how the program stores the data that you plan on entering. Moreover, you should understand how to carefully plan a database before you actually define it.

THE ORGANIZATION OF A DATABASE

When you use a database management program to enter information, it is stored in a file. The information you enter must be organized so that the program can easily manipulate it. To understand how a program manages information, you must first understand the five levels of organization used to store and manipulate data (Figure 12):

FIGURE 12   Levels of Data Organization.   When you enter data into a database management program, you enter it into fields. One or more of these fields make up a record. A record is like an index card; it contains all the information about a product, person, or other item. A field is a piece of the information in a record, for example, a name, an address, a phone number, or a price. Records are stored together in a file. If the files are related to each other, they comprise a database.

A. Alphanumeric characters are what you type
B. Fields contain specific pieces of information
C. Records contain one or more fields
D. Files contain one or more records
E. Databases contain one or more files

A.

ID	LASTNAME	FIRST	STREET	CITY	ST	ZIP	AREA	PHONE
1								

B.

ID	LASTNAME	FIRST	STREET	CITY	ST	ZIP	AREA	PHONE
101								

C.

ID	LASTNAME	FIRST	STREET	CITY	ST	ZIP	AREA	PHONE
101	June	Gary	100 Elm Street	New Haven	CT	10000	203	555-1000

D.

ID	LASTNAME	FIRST	STREET	CITY	ST	ZIP	AREA	PHONE
101	June	Gary	100 Elm Street	New Haven	CT	10000	203	555-1000
102	Benjamin	Nancy	25 Oak Street	Cambridge	MA	20000	617	555-1212

E.

ID	LASTNAME	FIRST	STREET	CITY	ST	ZIP	AREA	PHONE
101	June	Gary	100 Elm Street	New Haven	CT	10000	203	555-1000
102	Benjamin	Nancy	25 Oak Street	Cambridge	MA	20000	617	555-1212

ID	DATE	AMOUNT
101	6/8/88	10.00
102	6/9/88	15.00

A. When you enter information into a computer, you type it in from the keyboard. The first level of organization is, therefore, the alphanumeric characters you type, for example, numbers, and letters.

B. You use one or more characters to enter fields, for example, a person's ID or name. Fields can contain numbers (101), names (June), names and numbers (100 Elm Street), or formulas (100*3).

C. Related fields are stored together as records, for example, one person's ID, last name, first name, street, city, state, ZIP code, area code, and phone number.

D. Related records are stored together as files, for example, a list of customers.

E. Related files are stored together as a database. The database contains interrelated files that can be combined or from which information can be drawn.

As you have seen, relational databases can be thought of as interrelated tables of information. Each table should have a field containing key attributes that uniquely identify the records in the table. The field containing these key attributes is used to link the files in the database. There are many kinds of key attributes; for example, those used to uniquely identify persons include:

- Social security numbers
- Vehicle license numbers
- Driver's license numbers
- Bank account numbers
- Employee serial numbers
- Purchase order numbers
- Telephone numbers
- Credit card numbers
- Policy numbers
- Dates and times
- Account numbers

PLANNING YOUR DATABASE FILES

When you design a database, it is important to carefully consider the fields it will contain. These fields will become the elements for each record in the database. Choose fields that can describe each record. If possible, be sure that at least one field is unique so that records can be differentiated from one another. This unique field is called the key field and contains the key attributes discussed earlier.

You should also be sure to break down the fields so that you can later access and manipulate the data. In many cases, you might divide certain basic information into more than one field so that you can manipulate it more easily. For example, if you used only one field for both the persons' first and last names, and then entered names like John Smith, Betty Lewis, and Roger Wentworth, your file would be limited. You could not sort names based on the persons' last names. You also might not be able to find the record. To sort the persons' names, you set up two fields, one for the first name and one for the last name. The same is true of addresses. For example, if you do not enter ZIP codes into a separate field, you will not be able to sort the records by ZIP codes.

Designing a relational database requires very careful planning because more than one file can be involved. Not only does each file need to be well planned, but the relationships between files must also be carefully thought through. Figure 13 shows the plan for a database that contains two files, one to manage a list of customer names and addresses and the other to manage charges that they make and the dates they were made.

33

FILE: NAMELIST

Attribute	Field Name	Type	Length	Decimals	Example
ID Number	ID	Character	3		
Last name	LASTNAME	Character	8		
First name	FIRST	Character	8		
Street address	STREET	Character	15		
City	CITY	Character	18		
State	ST	Character	2		
Zip code	ZIP	Character	5		
Area code	AREA	Character	3		
Phone number	PHONE	Character	8		

A.

FILE: AMOUNTS

Attribute	Field Name	Type	Length	Decimals	Example
ID Number	ID	Character	3		
Date of purchase	DATE	Date	8		
Amount purchased	AMOUNT	Numeric	6	2	

B.

FIGURE 13   Planning a Database.   When planning a database, you list the fields you want to include for each record. You then plan the name of each field, its type, and its width. If you want to be able to link the tables, one of the fields must be common to both files. For example, in this database we plan to have two files: one to list customer names, addresses, and phone numbers and another to list customer charges and the dates they were made. The common field, or key attribute, that links both files in the database is the ID field.

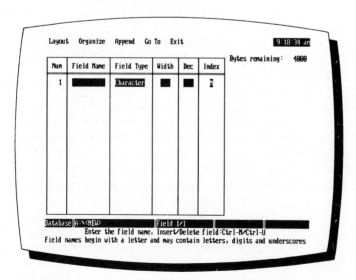

FIGURE 14 Database Design Screen.   When you highlight ⟨*create*⟩ and then press ENTER, the database design screen is displayed. The screen is organized like a table. Each row contains the description of a single record. Each column contains the fields that make up that record.

DEFINING A FILE

When you execute the command to create a new database file, the database design screen appears (Figure 14). You enter the definition of each field into the form using the cursor movement keys to move from field to field. If you make any mistakes, you can correct them with BACKSPACE or DEL. When you are finished defining the file, you use the program's command that saves the definition.

Field Number

The field number identifies the order in which the fields appear in the database. This number is assigned automatically. When entering fields, you should try to enter them in a sequence where the fields that will be used most often are entered first. This makes updating the database a little easier.

Field Names

When naming fields, you always use unique field names. The same field name cannot be used more than once in the same file. Typical field names might be LASTNAME, FIRST, STREET, CITY, STATE, ZIP, AREA, and PHONE. Besides being unique, field names must follow the rules described in Table 6.

TABLE 6   Field Name Rules

Number of characters	Between one and ten
First character	Must start with a letter
Other characters	The rest of the name can contain only letters, numbers, and underscore(_) characters
Spaces	Spaces are not allowed, but you can substitute underscores; for example, you cannot enter the field name LAST NAME, but you can enter LAST_NAME

Field Types

When you define a database field, you must specify the type of information that each field will contain. The available field types include the following:

- Character fields store all characters you can enter from the keyboard, including letters, numbers, symbols, and spaces. When numbers are entered into these fields, for example, ZIP codes or phone numbers, they are treated as text, not values. Numbers entered into these fields cannot be used in calculations.
- Numeric fields store values, including numbers, signs, and decimals. There are two kinds of numeric fields: integers (numbers without decimal places) and decimals. Numbers entered into these fields can be used in calculations.
- Float (short for floating point) fields are the same as numeric fields but are used mainly for scientific applications.
- Date fields store dates, which you can display in several formats. (The default format is MM/DD/YY.) When dates are entered in this field type, they can be used in calculations. Dates can be added and subtracted, or numbers can be added to or subtracted from them. This allows you to get answers to questions like, "What is the average number of days between orders?"
- Logical fields (sometimes called Boolean fields) are used to enter only true or false notations. For example, on dBASE, you enter true as T, t, Y, or y and false as F, f, N, or n.
- Memo fields are used to enter descriptive text, much as you would enter notes to yourself into a notebook. They are similar to character fields, but they can hold more text and are not used in some operations. Though all other fields are used for specific information, these fields are for general

35

information. You can enter notes about any of the other fields into the record, for example, a note that a price or address is expected to change and the date this is expected to happen.

Field Widths

When planning the file, you need to decide how many characters long each field has to be. Table 7 describes the field widths that dBASE allows. Deciding field widths ought not to be taken lightly. If you make the field too short, you will lose information. For instance, if you allowed only seven characters for the name, you could enter the name Smith but not the name Hamilton. But if you make the field too long, you waste memory and space on the disk used to store the file, limiting the number of fields in the record or the number of records in the file. Therefore, you need to balance the amount of information held with the space required to hold that information. To preserve memory, a memo field has a variable field width. As you enter text, the size of the field and the amount of memory or data storage space used increase automatically.

TABLE 7   Field Widths

Field Type	Widths (in characters)
Character fields	1-254
Numeric fields	1-20 (with 0-18 decimal places)
Float fields	1-20 (with 0-18 decimal places)
Date fields	8 (set automatically)
Logical fields	1 (set automatically)
Memo fields	10 (set automatically)

Decimals

The width of the field determines the number of characters that you can enter into it. If the field is numeric, you first specify the total number of digits in the number and then specify the number of decimal places. The program needs to know this so that it can store the values entered into these fields in a way that you can use them in calculations. When designating the width of numeric fields:

- Include room for a minus sign, the total number of characters, and a decimal point. For example, if you specify that the field is five characters long with two digits to the right of the decimal point, you can enter values from -9.99 to 99.99. You cannot enter numbers less than -9.99 (for example, -10.00) and greater than 99.99 (for example, 100.00) because they contain six characters.
- The maximum number of decimal places is always two less than the total width that you specify. For example, if you want 5 digits following the decimal point, you must set the width to at least 7 characters.

Index

When you define a new database, you can specify which fields the file is to be indexed on. This function is described in Topic 9, so you should ignore it here.

CATALOGS

One of the most useful features of dBASE IV is the catalog. A catalog is simply a collection of related files. For example, you might create a database, then create additional files that display selected information, design a form to use when entering data, or print a report or labels in a special format. As you do so, all the files associated with the database are displayed in the Control Center's panels when you open the catalog in which you have stored them.

To create a catalog, you first change the default drive and directory to the one you want to save your work in. If no catalog has been previously specified, all the files you create are saved in a catalog named UNTITLED.CAT. You can change the name of that catalog, or you can move other, already existing files into it. Once you have created a catalog, it is initially empty. However, all the files you create while a catalog is open are automatically stored in it.

You can also add files to or remove them from any catalog. When you remove a file from the catalog, it just removes its listing. The file itself is not erased from the disk unless you specify that it should be. Be careful with this command since you may want to use the file again. If you remove it from the catalog, you can use it again; if you erase it from the disk, you can't (unless you made a backup copy).

THE DATABASE'S STRUCTURE

When you define a database, you are giving it a structure. This structure includes all the field definitions that you enter on the database design screen. You can make a printout of this structure to refer to or file.

▼PROCEDURES

This section describes the procedures that you follow to:

- Change the default drive
- Create a new catalog
- Select or modify an existing catalog
- Define a database file
- Print out the database's structure

To Change the Default Drive

1. Press ALT-T to pull down the Tools menu.
2. Press D for *DOS utilities*.

 The Status Bar

When you are designing a database or are in Edit or Browse mode, the status bar at the bottom of the screen indicates the following information about the file:

- The type of screen displayed, for example, Database, Edit, or Browse.
- The name of the file, preceded by its path.
- The location of the cursor. For example, when defining a database, it may read *Field 3/4* to indicate that you are in the third field and there are four

fields. In Edit and Browse modes, it indicates the record number and the total number of records. For example, *Rec 2/3* indicates the current record is record 2 and there are 3 records.

- The source of the data, for example, a file or view.
- The status of the NUM LOCK (*Num*), CAPS LOCK (*Caps*), and INS (*Ins*) keys. If these indicators are displayed, the keys are currently engaged. To disengage them, press them again.

3. Press ALT-D to pull down the DOS menu.
4. Press S for *Set default drive:directory*, and the prompt reads *Drive:directory:*.
5. Type the letter of the drive that contains the database catalog and files, and then press ENTER. (You can also specify a directory.) If an entry is already listed, you can edit it or press CTRL-Y to delete it before entering your own.
6. Press ALT-E to pull down the Exit menu.
7. Press E for *Exit to Control Center*.

To Create a New Catalog

1. Press ALT-C to pull down the Control Center's Catalog menu.
2. Press U for *Use a different catalog* to display a list of available catalogs, if any.
3. Highlight *<create>*, and then press ENTER. The prompt reads *Enter name for new catalog:*.
4. Type the new catalog's name (see Table 8), and then press ENTER. The new catalog is opened, and its name is listed on the current catalog section of the Control Center.

TABLE 8   Catalog Names

Length	1 to 8 characters
Characters	Letters, numbers, and the underscore
Case	Uppercase or lowercase (lowercase letters are automatically converted to uppercase)

To Move an Existing File into a Catalog

1. Press ALT-C to pull down the Control Center's Catalog menu.
2. Press A for *Add file to catalog* to display a list of fields on the disk in the default drive/directory.
3. Highlight the file you want to add, and then press ENTER. The prompt reads *Edit the description of this .dbf file.*
4. Type a description, and then press ENTER. The file's name is listed on the Control Center.

To Specify or Modify Existing Catalogs

1. Press ALT-C to pull down the Control Center's Catalog menu.
2. Select any of the menu choices described in Table 9.

To Define a Database File

1. Highlight *<create>* in the Control Center's Data panel, and then press ENTER to display the database design screen (Figure 14).
2. Enter the description of each field in the file into the columns of this screen. Table 10 describes the commands to move the cursor around the screen, and Table 11 describes the commands to edit field definitions.
   • You must fill in the Field Name and Field Type for each field. If you try to move the highlight out of one of these fields without entering data, the computer beeps.
   • If you specify Character, Numeric, or Float field type, you must specify a

TABLE 9   Catalog Menu Commands

Command	Description
Use a different catalog	Displays a list of available catalogs on the default drive/directory. To select one, highlight its name, and then press ENTER.
Modify catalog name	Displays a prompt box into which you type the new name or edit an existing one, and then press ENTER.
Edit description of catalog	Displays a prompt box with the current catalog description, if any. You can enter a new description or edit the existing one, and then press ENTER.
Add file to catalog	Displays a list of available files on the default drive/directory. To add one to the catalog, highlight its name, and then press ENTER.
Remove highlighted catalog from file	Displays a prompt box asking if you want to remove the highlighted file from the catalog. To do so, press Y. You are then asked if you want to delete the file from the disk. (*Be careful since answering yes will permanently delete the file!*)
Change description of highlighted file	Displays a prompt box with the current database description, if any. You can enter a new description or edit the existing one, and then press ENTER.

TABLE 10   Database Design Navigation Commands

To Move the Highlight	Press
Up or down one line	↑ or ↓
Within a column	→ or ↓
To the next column	TAB or ENTER
To the previous column	BACKTAB
To the last column	END
To the first column	HOME

TABLE 11   Database Design Editing Commands

To	Press
Turn insert mode on and off	INS
Delete the character highlighted by the cursor	DEL
Delete the character to the left of the cursor	BACKSPACE
Delete the characters to the right of the cursor	CTRL-Y or CTRL-T
Insert field above one containing the cursor	CTRL-N
Delete field containing the cursor	CTRL-U
Exit field definition and save definition	CTRL-END

width. If you try to move the highlight out of the width field without specifying one, the computer beeps.
- If you specify Date, Memo, or Logical field type, widths are automatically assigned.
- If you specify Numeric or Float, you can enter the number of decimal places. Leaving this column blank sets the number to 0.

3. After defining the fields, press ALT-L to pull down the Layout menu, and then press E for *Edit database description* to display a prompt box.
4. Type a description of the database file, and then press ENTER. (The description is displayed in the file description area when you highlight the file's name on the Control Center.)
5. Press ALT-E to pull down the Exit menu, and then press S for *Save changes and exit*. The prompt reads *Save as:*.
6. Type a filename, and then press ENTER to return to the Control Center.

To Print Out the Database's Structure

1. Highlight the database's name on the Control Center's Data panel.
2. Press SHIFT-F2 to display the database design screen, and the Organize menu is automatically pulled down.
3. Press ← to pull down the Layout menu, and then press P for *Print database structure*. A submenu is displayed.
4. Press B for *Begin printing*.
5. Press ALT-E to pull down the Exit menu, and then press A for *Abandon changes and exit*.

▼TIPS

➤ **You can remove a file from the catalog** by highlighting its name and then pressing DEL.

➤ **After defining a file,** you can also save it by pressing CTRL-END (or CTRL-W).

TUTORIAL 4A
Defining a Data File for Names and Addresses

In this tutorial, you define a file that stores names, addresses, and phone numbers. To begin this tutorial, you must load the program as described in Topic 2. Figure 13A shows the plan for the database you will create in this tutorial.

Step 1 **Change the Default Drive.** You are probably saving your files on a floppy disk. Insert the floppy disk that you save your work on into drive A, and then change the default drive to that drive.

To change the default drive

Press	ALT-T to pull down the Tools menu
Press	D for *DOS Utilities* to display a list of files on the default drive
Press	ALT-D to pull down the DOS menu
Press	S for *Set default drive:directory*, and the prompt reads *Drive:Directory*. (Press CTRL-Y to delete any current entry.)
Type	**A:** and then press ENTER
Press	ALT-E to pull down the Exit menu
Press	E for *Exit to Control Center* to return to the Control Center

Result.   The default drive is now set to drive A. This path is listed on the current catalog line above the panels.

Step 2 **Create a Catalog.** dBASE's catalog is used to group together related files. Since you will be creating a number of related files in this part, let's create a catalog in which they can all be stored together.

To create a catalog

Press	ALT-C to pull down the Catalog menu
Press	U for *Use a different catalog* to display a list of existing catalog names, if any
Highlight	*<create>* in the submenu, and then press ENTER. The prompt reads *Enter name for new catalog:*
Type	**MYFILES** and then press ENTER

Result.   The current catalog section of the Control Center now reads *A:\MYFILES.CAT.* dBASE automatically entered the extension to the catalog name.

Step 3 **Add a Catalog Description.** After creating a catalog, you can add a line describing it.

To add a description line

Press	ALT-C to pull down the Catalog menu
Press	E for *Edit description of catalog*, and the prompt reads *Edit the description of this .cat file*
Type	**This catalog contains files belonging to** and then enter your name
Press	ENTER to return to the Control Center

Result.   The Control Center reappears.

Step 4 **Display the Description.** Now, let's display the description.

To display the catalog description

Press	ALT-C to pull down the catalog menu
Press	U for *Use a different catalog*

41

Result. A list of catalogs is displayed. Highlight MYFILES.CAT, and a box displays the description that you just entered. Press Esc twice to return to the Control Center.

Step 5 **Create a New Database File.** Now, display the database design screen so that you can create a database file.

To create a new file

Highlight   <*create*> on the Data panel, and then press ENTER to display the database design screen

Result. The drive spins, and in a moment, the database design screen appears (Figure 14).

- In the upper right-hand corner, an indicator shows how many bytes of memory are available for your file.
- Across the center of the screen are six columns with headings used to define fields. The cursor is blinking in the first column labeled *Field Name.*
- The status bar at the bottom of the screen displays the current command (*Database*), the default drive, the name of the file you are working on (<*NEW*>), and the position of the cursor by field. The indicator *1/1* indicates you are on the first field of 1.

Step 6 **Define a New Database File.** Before you can enter data into a file, you must define it by specifying field names, types, and widths. When you start, the cursor should be at the left of the highlight below the *Field Name* label. The number (1) at the far left indicates which field you are defining.

To enter field definitions, type the field name, and then press ENTER or TAB to move the cursor to the next description for the field. All field names are displayed in uppercase characters regardless of the case you enter them in. If you make a mistake, you will have a chance to correct it in the next step.

To define the first field

Type   **ID** and then press ENTER to move the cursor to the Field Type column

Press   C (for *Character*—the default field type), and the cursor automatically moves to the *Width* column

Type   **3** and then press ENTER. The cursor automatically moves to the *Index* column

Press   ENTER to begin a new field definition

To define the second field

Type   **LASTNAME** and then press ENTER to move the cursor to the *Field Type* column

Press   C (for *Character*), and the cursor automatically moves to the *Width* column

Type   **8** and then press ENTER. The cursor automatically moves to the *Index* column

Press   ENTER to begin a new field definition

To define the third field

Type   **FIRST** and then press ENTER to move the cursor to the *Field Type* column

Press   C (for *Character*), and the cursor automatically moves to the *Width* column

Type   **8** and then press ENTER. The cursor automatically moves to the *Index* column

Press   ENTER to begin a new field definition

To define the fourth field

Type	**STREET** and then press ENTER to move the cursor to the *Field Type* column
Press	C (for *Character*), and the cursor automatically moves to the *Width* column
Type	**15** and then press ENTER. The cursor automatically moves to the *Index* column
Press	ENTER to begin a new field definition

To define the fifth field

Type	**CITY** and then press ENTER to move the cursor to the *Field Type* column
Press	C (for *Character*), and the cursor automatically moves to the *Width* column
Type	**10** and then press ENTER. The cursor automatically moves to the *Index* column
Press	ENTER to begin a new field definition

To define the sixth field

Type	**ST** and then press ENTER to move the cursor to the *Field Type* column
Press	C (for *Character*), and the cursor automatically moves to the *Width* column
Type	**2** and then press ENTER. The cursor automatically moves to the *Index* column
Press	ENTER to begin a new field definition

To define the seventh field

Type	**ZIP** and then press ENTER to move the cursor to the *Field Type* column
Press	C (for *Character*), and the cursor automatically moves to the *Width* column
Type	**5** and then press ENTER. The cursor automatically moves to the *Index* column
Press	ENTER to begin a new field definition

To define the eighth field

Type	**AREA** and then press ENTER to move the cursor to the *Field Type* column
Press	C (for *Character*), and the cursor automatically moves to the *Width* column
Type	**3** and then press ENTER. The cursor automatically moves to the *Index* column
Press	ENTER to begin a new field definition

To define the ninth field

Type	**PHONE** and then press ENTER to move the cursor to the *Field Type* column
Press	C (for *Character*), and the cursor automatically moves to the *Width* column
Type	**8** and then press ENTER. The cursor automatically moves to the *Index* column

Result. Your results should match those in Figure 15.

Step 7   **Edit File Definitions.** Carefully compare your entries with those shown in Figure 15. If you find any errors, move the cursor to the *Field Name*, *Field Type*, or *Width* field using the cursor movement keys described in Table 10. Correct any mistakes using the editing keys described in Table 11.

43

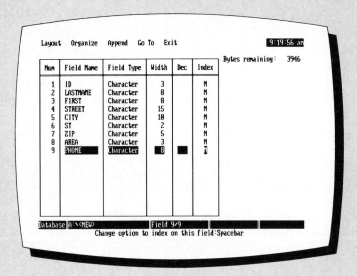

FIGURE 15 The Defined NAME-LIST Screen. When you have finished defining the NAMELIST file, your screen should look like this.

Step 8 **Add a Description.** When you create a database file, you can add a description that helps you identify its contents.

To add a description

Press ALT-L to pull down the Layout menu
Press E for *Edit database description*, and the prompt reads *Edit the description of this .dbf file*
Type **List of customer names and addresses** and then press ENTER

Result. The database design screen reappears.

Step 9 **Save the Definitions.** When you have finished making corrections, save the file. Be sure a formatted disk is in drive A.

To save the definition

Press ALT-E to pull down the Exit menu
Press S for *Save changes and exit*, and the prompt reads *Save as:*
Type **NAMELIST** and then press ENTER

Result. The Control Center reappears, and the new database file is listed in the Data panel. It is listed above the ruled line to indicate that the file is open and in memory. This means it is the current file when you execute other commands. The description you entered is displayed in the current file and description area when *NAMELIST* is highlighted in the Data panel.

Step 10 **Edit the Database Definition.** Now that you have defined the file, let's display it again, the way you would if you wanted to edit the definition.

To display a file's structure

Press SHIFT-F2 to display the database design screen, and the *Organize* menu is automatically pulled down
Press Esc to remove the Organize menu

Result. The information on the screen shows the definition you entered. Press ALT-E to pull down the Exit menu, and then press A for *Abandon changes and exit* to return to the Control Center.

Step 11 **Print the Database Structure.** You can print out a listing of the fields in the database. Before proceeding, be sure your printer is on.

44

To print the database structure

Press   SHIFT-F2 to display the database design screen, and the Organize menu is automatically pulled down

Press   ← to pull down the Layout menu, and then press P for *Print database structure* to display a submenu

Press   B for *Begin printing*

Press   ALT-E pull down the Exit menu, and then press A for *Abandon changes and exit*

Result.   The structure of the database is printed out.

Step 12   **Continue or Quit.** You have now completed this tutorial. Either continue with the next tutorial or quit the program.

TUTORIAL 4B
Defining a Data File for Amounts

In this tutorial, you define a database file that stores customer charges. To begin this tutorial, you must load the program as described in Topic 2. Figure 13B shows the plan for the database you will create in this tutorial.

Step 1   **Change the Default Drive.** You are probably saving your files on a floppy disk. Insert the floppy disk that you save your work on into drive A, and then change the default drive to that drive.

To change the default drive

Press   ALT-T to pull down the Tools menu

Press   D for *DOS Utilities* to display a list of files on the default drive

Press   ALT-D to pull down the DOS menu

Press   S for *Set default drive:directory*, and the prompt reads *Drive:Directory*. (Press CTRL-Y to delete any current entry.)

Type   **A:** and then press ENTER

Press   ALT-E to pull down the Exit menu

Press   E for *Exit to Control Center* to return to the Control Center

Result.   The default drive is now set to drive A. If you inserted the disk you used in Tutorial 4A, the MYFILES catalog is automatically listed. The current catalog section of the Control Center now reads *A:\MYFILES.CAT*.

Step 2   **Create a New Database File.** Now, let's display the database design screen so that you can create a database file.

To create a new file named NAMELIST

Highlight   *<create>* on the Data panel, and then press ENTER to display the database design screen

Result.   The drive spins, and in a moment, the database design screen appears (Figure 14).

Step 3   **Define a New Database File.** In the NAMELIST file, all fields were defined as character fields. Here, you specify another character field but also add a date and numeric field. If you make a mistake, you will have a chance to correct it in the next step.

45

To define the first field

Type	**ID** and then press ENTER to move the cursor to the *Field Type* highlight
Press	C (for *Character*), and the cursor automatically moves to the *Width* highlight
Type	**3** and then press ENTER. The cursor automatically moves to the *Index* column
Press	ENTER to begin a new field definition

To define the second field

Type	**DATE** and then press ENTER to move the cursor to the *Field Type* highlight
Press	SPACEBAR repeatedly to cycle through the available field types
Press	SPACEBAR until the field type displays *Date*
Press	ENTER and the cursor automatically moves to the *Index* column
Press	ENTER to begin a new field definition

To define the third field

Type	**AMOUNT** and then press ENTER to move the cursor to the *Field Type* highlight
Press	N (for *Numeric*), and the cursor automatically moves to the *Width* highlight
Type	**6** and then press ENTER to move the cursor to the *Dec* highlight
Type	**2** and then press ENTER to move the cursor to the *Index* column

Result. Your results should match those in Figure 16.

Step 4 **Edit File Definitions.** Carefully compare your entries with those shown in Figure 16. If you find any errors, move the cursor to the *Field Name*, *Field Type*, or *Width* field using the commands described in Table 10. Type over the mistakes, or use the editing keys described in Table 11.

Step 5 **Save the Definitions.** When you have finished making corrections, save the file.

To save the definition

Press	ALT-E to pull down the Exit menu
Press	S for *Save changes and exit*, and the prompt reads *Save as:*
Type	**AMOUNTS** and then press ENTER

FIGURE 16 The Defined AMOUNTS Screen. When you have finished defining the AMOUNTS file, your screen should look like this.

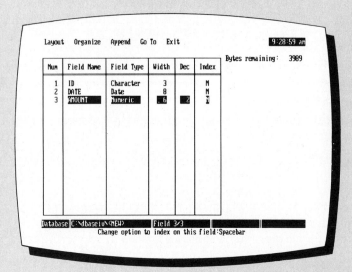

Result. The Control Center reappears, and the new database file is listed in the Data panel.

Step 6 **Add a Description.** You can enter or edit a field's description after you have saved the file.

To add a file description

Press	SHIFT-F2 to display the database design screen, and the Organize menu is automatically pulled down
Press	← to pull down the Layout menu
Press	E for *Edit database description*, and the prompt reads *Edit the description of this .dbf file*
Type	**List of customer charges** and then press ENTER

To save the description

Press	ALT-E to pull down the Exit menu
Press	S for *Save changes and exit*

Result. The Control Center reappears. The description you entered is displayed in the current file and description area when *AMOUNTS* is highlighted in the Data panel.

Step 7 **Print the Database Structure.** Before proceeding, be sure your printer is on.

To print the database structure

Press	SHIFT-F2 to display the database design screen
Press	ALT-L to pull down the Layout menu, and then press P for *Print database structure* to display a submenu
Press	B for *Begin printing*
Press	ALT-E pull down the Exit menu, and then press A for *Abandon changes and exit*

Result. The structure of the database is printed out, and the Control Center is displayed.

Step 8 **Continue or Quit.** You have now completed this tutorial. Either continue with the next tutorial or quit the program.

▼**EXERCISES**

EXERCISE 4A   Define a Database for a Course Schedule

Define a database for the courses shown in Figure 17. Before doing so, plan the database using the grid below. Enter the name, type, and width that you will specify for each field.

Note. All the day fields—MON, TUE, and so on—are logical fields.

Attribute	Course #	Title	Time	MON	TUE	WED	THU	FRI	SAT
Field Name									
Field Type									
Field Width									

NUMBER	TITLE	TIME	MON	TUE	WED	THU	FRI	SAT
ACC101	Introduction to Accounting	8:00am	Y	N	Y	N	Y	N
MGT102	Business Management	10:00am	Y	N	Y	N	Y	N
CPS101	Computer Applications	1:00pm	N	Y	N	Y	N	Y
ENG101	English Composition	9:00am	N	Y	N	Y	N	Y
HIS101	US History	3:00pm	N	Y	N	Y	N	Y

FIGURE 17   The COURSES Database.

After you plan the database, display the database design screen, and then define the file. When you are finished, save it as COURSES, and then return to the Control Center. It should be listed in your MYFILES catalog on the data panel. If it isn't, add it to the catalog. Add a description to the file identifying it as a course schedule. Make a printout of the file's structure. You will enter data into the file in Exercise 5A.

EXERCISE 4B   Add the PLACEST File to the MYFILES Catalog

The *Resource Disk* that accompanies this text includes a file named PLACEST.DBF that contains records compiled by the U.S. Bureau of the Census. You will be using this file in many of the following exercises, so add it to your MYFILES catalog. If it is not on the data disk that you are using, copy it to that disk from the *Resource Disk*. When you add the file to the catalog, you will be prompted to enter a description. Type **Census file from the U.S. Bureau of the Census.** Make a printout of the file's structure.

This database includes the fields of information described in Table 12.

TABLE 12   The Census Database

Field	Description
STATE	FIPS state code
AREANAME	Area name
POP01080	Population April 1, 1980
POP01086	Population July 1, 1986 (estimate)
PCI01079	Per capita income 1979
PCI01085	Per capita income 1985
POP13086	Population percent change 1980-1986
PCI11085	Per capita income, percent change 1979-1985

QUESTIONS

1. List the five levels of data in a database.
2. What is a key field? Why is it important?
3. Why would you not be able to sort names based on last names if you entered both first and last names into one field?

4. Briefly describe each of the following types of fields:
   Character
   Numeric
   Logical
   Date
   Memo
5. Why not specify the maximum width available for each field so that you do not have to plan field widths so carefully?
6. What width would you specify for a field into which the largest number you were going to enter was 100.00? 10.00? 1000.00?
7. What is a catalog? What does it display?
8. What is the database structure? How can you make a printout of it?

TOPIC 5
Entering Records

▼CONCEPTS

Once a database has been designed, you are ready to begin entering records into it.

OPENING THE DATABASE FILE

To enter records, you must first perform two steps:

1. Specify the catalog to be used. This displays all the database files in the catalog on the Data panel of the Control Center's work surface. When you load dBASE, the catalog that you were using when you quit your last session is automatically retrieved if it is in the default drive and directory. If the catalog is not in the default drive and directory, you have to change the default, and then the previously used catalog is retrieved. You can also specify any other catalog that you want to use.
2. Move the highlight to the Data panel, highlight the name of the database you want to enter data into, and then press F2. This retrieves the database file from the disk into the computer's memory and displays the Edit or Browse screens.

ENTERING RECORDS

When entering data, you can do so using either the Edit or Browse screens. These screens show two views of the same database, and they are closely linked. Once you have entered at least one record, you can press F2 to switch back and forth between them. Each time you press F2, the other screen is displayed.

- The Edit screen (Figure 18) shows all the fields in one record. This is the preferred view if a file contains many fields. If there are too many fields to fit on the screen at one time, you can press PgDn and PgUp to display additional fields. You can also design a form for this view that makes data entry easier and makes the screen more attractive.

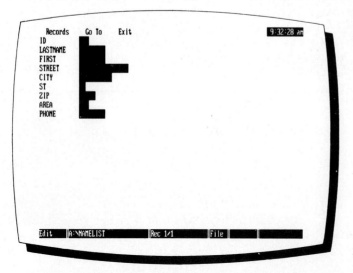

FIGURE 18   The Edit Screen. The Edit screen shows all fields in a single record.

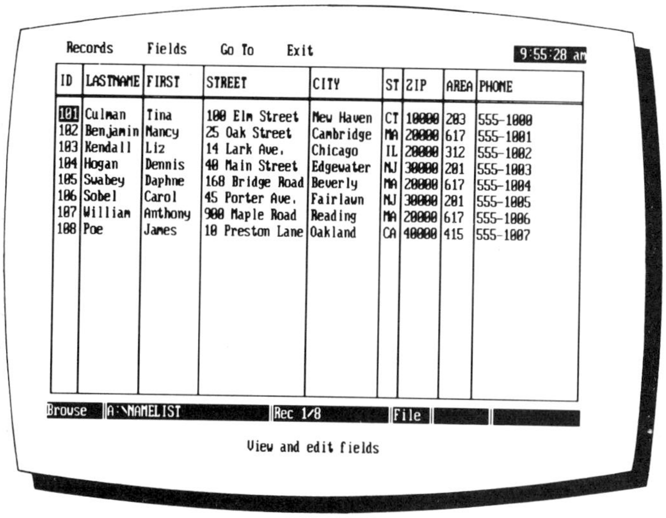

FIGURE 19   **The Browse Screen.**   The Browse screen shows a number of records.

- The Browse screen (Figure 19) shows a group of records arranged in a table. Records are on rows, and fields are in columns. This is the preferred mode when you want to work on many records at the same time. Its only drawback is that if the file contains too many fields, you may have to scroll the screen horizontally to see them. (You cannot switch to the Browse screen from the Edit screen until you have entered at least one record.)

On either the Edit or Browse screen, when you move the cursor back through records that you have entered, you are no longer in enter mode. You can enter records by moving the highlight to the last record on the Browse screen or the last field in the last record on the Edit screen and then pressing ↓ . This displays the prompt ===> *Add new records? (Y/N)*. Press Y to add new records.

You can enter records in any order you want. There is no need to worry about the order because you can sort the file into any desired order after you enter the records. The number of records you can enter is determined by the size of each record and the program's limitations. You will not run out of space for your records. dBASE IV can hold 1 billion records (or 2 billion characters), although an educational version is available that limits your records to about a hundred or more.

When entering data, be sure to use the correct keys. Do not use a lowercase l (the letter ell) for 1 (the number one) or the letter O for the number 0 (zero). If you do, you may have problems working with the data later.

SAVING RECORDS

Records are saved automatically when you move the highlight to a new record after entering them.

PRINTING QUICK REPORTS

Any time you are working on a database file and the Control Center, Browse, or Edit screen is displayed, you can press SHIFT-F9, then press B for *Begin printing* to print out a listing of the records contained in the database file. Since these printouts are not formatted, they are called quick reports.

51

▼PROCEDURES

This section describes the procedures that you follow to:

- Open an existing catalog
- Open a database file
- Enter data into a database file
- Print a quick report

To Open an Existing Catalog

1. Press ALT-C to pull down the Control Center's Catalog menu.
2. Press U for *Use a different catalog* to display a list of available catalogs.
3. Highlight the name of the catalog that you want to open, and then press ENTER. The new catalog is opened, and its name is listed on the current catalog line of the Control Center.

To Open a Database File

1. Highlight the name of the database file in the Control Center's Data panel.
2. Press ENTER to retrieve the file. Its name is listed above the horizontal bar in the panel.

To Enter Data in an Open Database File

1. Press F2 to display the Edit screen (Figure 18). You can also press F2 to display the Browse screen if the database contains at least one record.
2. Type in your data using the commands described in Table 13 to move the highlight and any of the commands in Table 14 to edit your entries.

TABLE 13   Edit/Browse Screen Navigation Commands

To	Press
Move Between Fields	
Move to the next field	TAB, F4, or ENTER
Move to the previous field	BACKTAB or F3
Move Between Records	
Move the cursor up one field (Edit) or one record (Browse)	↑
Move the cursor down one field (Edit) or one record (Browse)	↓
Display the previous screen, if any	PGUP
Display the next screen, if any	PGDN
Move to the first field (Browse) or the beginning of the field (Edit)	HOME
Move to the last field (Browse) or the end of the field (Edit)	END
Move to the same field in first record	CTRL-PGUP
Move to the same field in last record	CTRL-PGDN

TABLE 14 Edit/Browse Screen Entering and Editing Commands

To	Press
Switch between insert and typeover modes	INS
Move the cursor left or right one character	← or →
Move to the beginning of the next word	CTRL-→
Move to the beginning of the previous word	CTRL-←
Delete the character above the cursor	DEL
Delete the character to the left of the cursor	BACKSPACE
Delete from the cursor to the beginning of the next word	CTRL-T
Delete from the cursor to the end of the field	CTRL-T
Copy data from the same field in the previous record	SHIFT-F8
Open a memo field	F3 or F4
Enlarge or shrink a memo field	F9
Move into a memo field	CTRL-HOME
Save the changes	CTRL-END
Exit without saving the changes to the current record	ESC

To Print a Quick Report

1. Highlight the name of the database on the Control Center's Data panel, or display the Browse or Edit screen.
2. Press SHIFT-F9 to display a submenu. (The choices on this menu are discussed in Table 32 in Topic 12.)
3. Press B for *Begin printing.*

TIP

► **If a blank page is ejected from the printer when you print quick reports, you can change a setting on the Print menu to change it.** Press SHIFT-F9 to display the Print menu. Then press C for *Control of Printer* to display a submenu. Press N for *New page* to cycle through the settings *AFTER, BEFORE, BOTH,* or *NONE.* With the setting where you want it, press ESC to leave the menu.

TUTORIAL 5A
Entering Records in the NAMELIST File

In this tutorial, you enter records using the Edit screen. This tutorial uses the NAMELIST database file you defined in Tutorial 4A. You must complete that tutorial before you can begin this one.

Step 1 **Open the NAMELIST File.** Before proceeding:

1. Load dBASE so that the Control Center is displayed.
2. Insert your data disk into drive A, and then change the default drive to drive A. (The current file and description section of the Control Center should read *A:\MYFILES.CAT*.)
3. Open the NAMELIST database so that its name is above the ruled line in the Control Center's Data panel. (To open a file, highlight its name on the Control Center, and then press ENTER twice.)

If you need help, refer to Step 1 in Tutorial 4A.

Step 2 **Enter Records.** Now, enter data into the file.

To enter records into the file

Press   F2 to display the Edit screen

Result.   The Edit screen displays a blank entry form (Figure 18). The first column lists the field names you defined in the previous topic. The second column contains highlights that indicate the width of the fields that you specified. To enter data into the file, refer to the following three steps and Figure 20, on page 55.

1. Type in the data exactly as shown in Figure 20. Uppercase and lowercase letters are important because you will look for data, and the program is case sensitive. For example, if you enter KENDALL, and later search for Kendall, the program will not find it. If you make a mistake when entering data, press BACKSPACE to delete it, and then correctly reenter it.
2. After you complete a field entry, press ENTER or TAB to move the cursor to the next field. If the number of characters you enter equals the field width, the computer beeps, and the cursor automatically moves to the next field.
3. When you enter data into the last field (PHONE), it fills the field. Then the computer beeps, a new blank record is automatically displayed, and the previous record is saved onto the disk.

Step 3 **Edit the Records.** After completing all eight records, press PGUP and PGDN to scroll through them. (If you press PGDN when the last record is displayed, and the prompt reads ===> *Add new records? (Y/N)*, press N.) Carefully compare your data with Figure 20. (You can press F2 to display the Browse screen to make your comparison easier.) If there are any mistakes, use the keys described in Table 13 to move the cursor and the editing commands described in Table 14 to correct any mistakes. It is important that the records be entered correctly. If they are not, you may have problems in the following tutorials.

Step 4 **Save the Records.** When entering records, they are automatically saved onto the disk when you move to the next record. But to be sure the last record is saved, when you have finished making corrections, save the file and return to the Control Center.

To save the file

Press   ALT-E to pull down the Exit menu

Press   E for *Exit*

Record 1:			**Record 2:**	
ID:	101		ID:	102
LASTNAME:	Culman		LASTNAME:	Benjamin
FIRST:	Tina		FIRST:	Nancy
STREET:	100 Elm Street		STREET:	25 Oak Street
CITY:	New Haven		CITY:	Cambridge
ST:	CT		ST:	MA
ZIP:	10000		ZIP:	20000
AREA:	203		AREA:	617
PHONE:	555-1000		PHONE:	555-1001
Record 3:			**Record 4:**	
ID:	103		ID:	104
LASTNAME:	Kendall		LASTNAME:	Hogan
FIRST:	Liz		FIRST:	Dennis
STREET:	14 Lark Ave.		STREET:	40 Main Street
CITY:	Chicago		CITY:	Edgewater
ST:	IL		ST:	NJ
ZIP:	20000		ZIP:	30000
AREA:	312		AREA:	201
PHONE:	555-1002		PHONE:	555-1003
Record 5:			**Record 6:**	
ID:	105		ID:	106
LASTNAME:	Swabey		LASTNAME:	Sobel
FIRST:	Daphne		FIRST:	Carol
STREET:	168 Bridge Road		STREET:	45 Porter Ave.
CITY:	Beverly		CITY:	Fairlawn
ST:	MA		ST:	NJ
ZIP:	20000		ZIP:	30000
AREA:	617		AREA:	201
PHONE:	555-1004		PHONE:	555-1005
Record 7:			**Record 8:**	
ID:	107		ID:	108
LASTNAME:	Anthony		LASTNAME:	Poe
FIRST:	William		FIRST:	James
STREET:	900 Maple Road		STREET:	10 Preston Lane
CITY:	Reading		CITY:	Oakland
ST:	MA		ST:	CA
ZIP:	20000		ZIP:	40000
AREA:	617		AREA:	415
PHONE:	555-1006		PHONE:	555-1007

FIGURE 20 NAMELIST File Records. This figure shows the eight records that you enter into the NAMELIST file.

Result. The database file is saved onto the disk, and the Control Center reappears.

Step 5 **Print Out the Records.** Print out a list of the records so that you can check it more carefully. Before proceeding, be sure that the printer is ready.

To print out the records

    Press   SHIFT-F9 to display a submenu
    Press   B for *Begin printing*

Result. The records you entered are printed out. Carefully compare your print-out with the data shown in Figure 20.

55

Step 6 **Continue or Quit.** You have now completed this tutorial. Either continue with the next tutorial or quit the program.

TUTORIAL 5B
Entering Records in the AMOUNTS File

In this tutorial, you enter records into the AMOUNTS file using the Edit screen. This tutorial uses the AMOUNTS database file you created in Tutorial 4B. You must complete that tutorial before you can begin this one.

Step 1 **Open the AMOUNTS File.** Before proceeding:

1. Load dBASE so that the Control Center is displayed.
2. Insert your data disk into drive A, and then change the default drive to drive A. (The current file and description section of the Control Center should read *A:\MYFILES.CAT.*)
3. Open the AMOUNTS database so that its name is above the ruled line in the Control Center's Data panel.

If you need help, refer to Step 1 in Tutorial 4A.

Step 2 **Enter Records.** Now, enter data into the file.

To enter records into the file

Press   F2 to display a blank entry form

Result.   The Edit screen displays a blank entry form (Figure 21). Type in the data exactly as shown in Figure 22. You enter dates in the format MM/DD/YY. If you enter two digits for each part of the date, you do not have to enter the slashes. If you enter only one digit, you do have to enter the slashes. For example, you can enter the date June 8, 1990, as 060890 or 6/8/90.

FIGURE 21 The AMOUNTS Edit Screen. The Edit screen shows all fields in a single record.

Record 1:		Record 2:	
ID:	101	ID:	102
DATE:	06/08/90	DATE:	06/09/90
AMOUNT:	10.00	AMOUNT:	15.00
Record 3:		Record 4:	
ID:	103	ID:	104
DATE:	06/10/90	DATE:	06/11/90
AMOUNT:	35.00	AMOUNT:	25.00
Record 5:		Record 6:	
ID:	105	ID:	106
DATE:	06/12/90	DATE:	06/13/90
AMOUNT:	20.00	AMOUNT:	50.00
Record 7:		Record 8:	
ID:	107	ID:	108
DATE:	06/14/90	DATE:	06/15/90
AMOUNT:	15.00	AMOUNT:	10.00

FIGURE 22 AMOUNTS File Records. This figure shows the eight records that you enter into the AMOUNTS file.

Step 3 **Edit the Records.** After completing all eight records, press PGUP and PGDN to scroll through them. (If you press PGDN when the last record is displayed, and the prompt reads ===> *Add new records? (Y/N)*, press N.) Carefully compare your data with Figure 22. (You can press F2 to display the Browse screen to make your comparison easier.) If there are any mistakes, use the keys described in Table 13 to move the cursor and the keys described in Table 14 to edit the mistakes.

Step 4 **Save the Records.** When entering records, they are automatically saved onto the disk when you move to the next record. But to be sure the last record is saved, when you have finished making corrections, save the file and return to the Control Center.

To save the file

Press   ALT-E to pull down the Exit menu, and then press E for *Exit*

Result.   The database file is saved onto the disk, and the Control Center reappears.

Step 5 **Print Out the Records.** Print out a list of the records so that you can check it more carefully. Before proceeding, be sure that the printer is ready.

To print out the records

Press   SHIFT-F9 to display a submenu
Press   B for *Begin printing*

Result.   The records you entered are printed out. Carefully compare your printout with the data shown in Figure 22.

Step 6 **Continue or Quit.** You have now completed this tutorial. Either continue with the next tutorial or quit the program.

▼ EXERCISES

EXERCISE 5A   Enter Records in the COURSES Database File

Open the COURSES file that you defined in Exercise 4A. Enter the records shown in Figure 17. When you are finished, save the file and print out a quick report.

EXERCISE 5B   Print Out the PLACEST File's Records

Print out a quick report of the PLACEST file's contents. If it does not all fit on a single page, you may be able to print it in compressed type. To do so, Press SHIFT-F9 to display the Print menu. Press C for *Control of printer* to display a submenu. Press T for *Text pitch* to cycle through the options *DEFAULT, PICA* (larger), *ELITE* (smaller), and *CONDENSED* (smallest). With the setting the way you want it, press Esc and then begin printing again. Table 12 describes the fields in the report.

▼ QUESTIONS

1. What is the first step when you want to enter data into a database file?
2. What two screens can you use to enter records? How do they differ? What key do you press to move between them?
3. In what order do you enter records?
4. When are records saved when you enter them into a file?
5. What is a quick report? How do you print one?

TOPIC 6
Displaying Records

▼ **CONCEPTS**

Once data have been entered into a database file, you generally work with specific records. For example, you may want to look up the phone number of John Davis, change the number of baseballs in inventory, delete a specific record, or change the data in one or more fields. To do this, you can browse though the records, much as you would flip through the cards in an index card file. If the file has just been created, the records will appear in the order they were entered in.

BROWSE/EDIT SCREEN COMMANDS

When you display the data in your database, you can press F2 to switch between the Edit and Browse screens. The screen that is displayed depends on which screen you were using the last time you viewed the file. The program remembers if you were looking at the Edit or Browse screen, and displays the same view. When either screen is displayed, you can use the navigation commands described in Table 13. You can also use the menu commands described in Table 14 to move the highlight to a specific record.

If, when you are looking at records on the Browse screen, there are too many fields to fit on the screen, you have to scroll the screen horizontally to see them. The *Lock Fields on left* choice on the Browse screen's Fields menu freezes the leftmost fields on the screen so that you can scroll a database that is wider than the screen and still be able to identify the records from the contents of the locked fields that do not scroll.

SEARCHING FOR RECORDS

Scrolling through a file to look at records one after another in the order they are stored or sorted can take a long time if the file has many records. When you have displayed records on the Browse or Edit screen, you can pull down the Go To menu and use its commands to go directly to the records that you want. Many of the commands go to the first or last record, or to a record that you specify by number. The menu also has three commands that you can use to search a field for a specific piece of data. When you use the search commands, you can search forward or backward through the file and limit or expand the search using wild-cards and matching capitalization.

▼ The Record Pointer

When you highlight a record on the Browse or Edit screen, it is called the current record. The current record is marked inside the file by a record pointer, which is not displayed on the screen. This record pointer always points to the current record. In this topic, and those that follow, the position of this record pointer determines the outcome of some commands. For example, if you use the *Skip* command on the Go To menu, the highlight skips records from the one pointed to by the record pointer. If you use the *Search forward* or *Search backward* command on the same menu, the file is searched from the current record.

- You can use wildcards to expand the search. The ? stands for a single character, and the * stands for any group of characters. For example, Sm?th finds Smith or Smyth, and Sm* finds Smith or Smithers. Searching for 01/??/90 in a date field finds all records from January 1990.
- You can use the Match capitalization command to limit the search.
  - When set to *YES*, the search is case sensitive. Searching for Smith finds Smith but not SMITH or smith.
  - When set to *NO*, the search is not case sensitive. Searching for Smith finds SMITH, Smith, or smith.

▼ PROCEDURES

This section describes the procedures that you follow to:

- Display records on the Browse or Edit screen
- Lock fields so they don't scroll off the Browse screen

To Display Specific Records

1. Highlight the name of the database you want to browse on the Control Center's Data panel.
2. Press F2. (To switch between the Edit and Browse screens, press F2.)
3. Either   use any of the commands described in Table 13 to scroll through the records displayed on the screen.

   Or   press ALT-G to pull down the Go To menu, and then select any of the menu choices described in Table 15. (If you are planning to use the Search commands, position the highlight in the field that you want to search before pressing ALT-G.)

TABLE 15   Go To Menu Commands

Command	Description
Top record	Moves the record pointer to the first record in the file.
Last record	Moves the record pointer to the last record in the file.
Record number	Moves the record pointer to the record number that you specify.
Skip	Skips the number of records you specify and moves the record pointer to the record that follows.
Index key search	Searches indexed files (see Topic 9).
Forward search	Searches the file in the field containing the cursor for the string that you specify toward the end of the file. When you select this command, the prompt reads *Enter search string:*.
	1. Type the search string, and then press ENTER. The highlight moves to the record that contains the string. If no match is found, the messages reads ** *Not Found* **. If that message appears, press any key to return to the Go To menu.
	2. After finding the string, press SHIFT-F4 to move the highlight to the next occurrence, or press SHIFT-F3 to move the highlight to the previous occurrence.
Backward search	Searches the file in the field containing the cursor for the string that you specify toward the beginning of the file (see *Forward search*).
Match capitalization	Specifies if the *Forward search* and *Backward search* commands should only highlight records that exactly match your string's capitalization or not.

4. When you are finished, press ALT-E to pull down the Exit menu, and then press E for *Exit* to return to the Control Center.

To Lock and Unlock Fields

1. Display the database file in Browse mode.
2. Press ALT-F to pull down the Fields menu, then press L for Lock fields on left. The prompt reads *Enter number of fields to remain stationary:*.
3. Type the number of fields that you want to keep from scrolling (enter 0 to unlock previously locked fields), and then press ENTER.

TIP

➤ **You can print a quick report when the Edit or Browse screen is displayed.** To do so, press SHIFT-F9, and then press B for *Begin printing.*

TUTORIAL 6A
Displaying Records in the NAMELIST File

In this tutorial, you display records in the NAMELIST database file you entered records into in Tutorial 5A. You must complete that tutorial before you can begin this one.

Step 1   **Open the NAMELIST File.** Before proceeding:

1. Load dBASE so that the Control Center is displayed.
2. Insert your data disk into drive A, and then change the default drive to drive A. (The current file and description section of the Control Center should read *A:\MYFILES.CAT*.)
3. Open the NAMELIST database so that its name is above the ruled line in the Control Center's Data panel.

Step 2   **Browse through Records.** When you enter records, the Edit screen displays them one at a time. However, you can press F2 whenever this screen is displayed to see the records on the Browse screen.

To browse through records in the file
> Press   F2 to display the Browse screen (if the Edit screen is displayed, press F2)

Result.   All the records are displayed on the screen (Figure 23). The highlight indicates which record is the current record as does the status bar. For example, *Rec 1/8* indicates that the highlight is on record 1 and the database contains 8 records.

Step 3   **Display Specific Records.** When records are displayed on the Browse screen, you can scroll the highlight through the records with the up and down arrow keys. This is fine when a database contains as few records as this one. However, with a large database, there are commands that allow you to quickly move the highlight to a specific file. As you execute the following commands, watch which record is highlighted, and watch the *Rec* indicator on the status bar.

To display the last record
> Press   ALT-G to pull down the Go To menu
> Press   L for *Last record*

```
   Records    Fields    Go To    Exit                        9:55:28 am
  ┌──┬────────┬───────┬───────────┬─────────┬──┬─────┬────┬────────┐
  │ID│LASTNAME│FIRST  │STREET     │CITY     │ST│ZIP  │AREA│PHONE   │
  ├──┼────────┼───────┼───────────┼─────────┼──┼─────┼────┼────────┤
  │101│Culman  │Tina   │100 Elm Street│New Haven│CT│10000│203 │555-1000│
  │102│Benjamin│Nancy  │25 Oak Street │Cambridge│MA│20000│617 │555-1001│
  │103│Kendall │Liz    │14 Lark Ave.  │Chicago  │IL│20000│312 │555-1002│
  │104│Hogan   │Dennis │40 Main Street│Edgewater│NJ│30000│201 │555-1003│
  │105│Swabey  │Daphne │160 Bridge Road│Beverly │MA│20000│617 │555-1004│
  │106│Sobel   │Carol  │45 Porter Ave.│Fairlawn │NJ│30000│201 │555-1005│
  │107│William │Anthony│900 Maple Road│Reading  │MA│20000│617 │555-1006│
  │108│Poe     │James  │10 Preston Lane│Oakland │CA│40000│415 │555-1007│
  └──┴────────┴───────┴───────────┴─────────┴──┴─────┴────┴────────┘

  Browse  A:\NAMELIST          Rec 1/8        File
                        View and edit fields
```

FIGURE 23   **The NAMELIST File on the Browse Screen.** Your NAMELIST file should look like this on the Browse screen.

To display the first record

Press ALT-G to pull down the Go To menu

Press T for *Top record*

To display record number 5

Press ALT-G to pull down the Go To menu

Press R for *Record number*, and the prompt reads *Enter record number:*

Type **5** and then press ENTER

To skip two records

Press ALT-G to pull down the Go To menu

Press S for *Skip*, and the prompt reads *Enter number of records to skip:*

Type **2** and then press ENTER

Result. Each command displays a specific record.

Step 4 **Search for a Record.** You can search for a record that has specified data in the field containing the cursor. To do so, you position the cursor in the field that you want to search, and then specify if the search is forward or backward.

To move the record pointer to the top of the file

Press ALT-G to pull down the Go To menu

Press T for *Top record*

To search for a record

Press TAB to move the cursor to the *ST* field

Press ALT-G to pull down the Go To menu

Press F for *Forward search*, and the prompt reads *Enter search string:*

Type **MA** and then press ENTER

Result. The first record with MA in the ST field is highlighted. Press SHIFT-F3 and SHIFT-F4 to move to the next occurrence and the previous occurrence. (If the prompt reads ** *Not Found* **, press any key to return to the Browse screen.) Press ALT-E to pull down the Exit menu, and then press E for *Exit* to return to the Control Center.

Step 5 **Continue or Quit.** You have now completed this tutorial. Either continue with the next tutorial or quit the program.

TUTORIAL 6B
Displaying Records in the AMOUNTS File

In this tutorial, you display records in the AMOUNTS database file you entered records into in Tutorial 5B. You must complete that tutorial before you can begin this one.

Step 1 **Open the AMOUNTS File.** Before proceeding:

1. Load dBASE so that the Control Center is displayed.
2. Insert your data disk into drive A, and then change the default drive to drive A. (The current file and description section of the Control Center should read *A:\MYFILES.CAT.*)

3. Open the AMOUNTS database so that its name is above the ruled line in the Control Center's Data panel.

Step 2   **Browse Through Records.** When you enter records, the Edit screen displays them one at a time. However, you can press F2 whenever this screen is displayed to display the Browse screen.

To browse through records in the file

Press   F2 to display the Browse screen (if the Edit screen is displayed, press F2)

Result.   All the records are displayed on the screen (Figure 24). The highlight indicates which record is the current record.

Step 3   **Display Specific Records.** As you execute the following commands, watch which record is highlighted.

To display the last record

Press   ALT-G to pull down the Go To menu
Press   L for *Last record*

To display the first record

Press   ALT-G to pull down the Go To menu
Press   T for *Top record*

To display record number 3

Press   ALT-G to pull down the Go To menu
Press   R for *Record number,* and the prompt reads Enter record number:
Type   **3** and then press ENTER

To skip two records

Press   ALT-G to pull down the Go To menu
Press   S for *Skip,* and the prompt reads *Enter number of records to skip:*
Type   **2** and then press ENTER

Result.   Each command displays a specific record.

Step 4   **Search for a Record.** You can search for a record that has specified data in the field containing the cursor. To do so, you position the cursor in the field that you want to search, and then specify if the search is forward or backward.

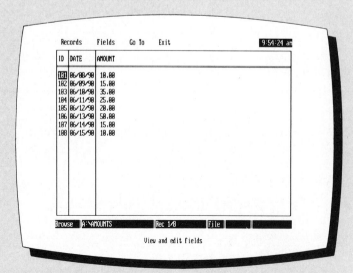

FIGURE 24   The AMOUNTS File on the Browse Screen. Your AMOUNTS file should look like this on the Browse screen.

To move the record pointer to the top of the file

| Press | ALT-G to pull down the Go To menu |
| Press | T for *Top record* |

To search for a record

Press	TAB to move the cursor to the *AMOUNT* field
Press	ALT-G to pull down the Go To menu
Press	F for *Forward search,* and the prompt reads *Enter search string:*
Type	**50.00** and then press ENTER

Result. The record with 50.00 in the AMOUNT field is highlighted. Press ALT-E to pull down the Exit menu, and then press E for *Exit* to return to the Control Center.

Step 5 Continue or Quit. You have now completed this tutorial. Either continue with the next tutorial or quit the program.

▼EXERCISES

EXERCISE 6A   Browse and Search the COURSES File

Display the COURSES file on the Browse screen. Use the *Forward search* and *Backward search* commands to find the course US History. Make record 4 the current record, and then press F2 to display the Edit screen. Which record is displayed?

EXERCISE 6B   Browse and Search the PLACEST File

Open the PLACEST.DBF file that you added to your catalog in Exercise 4B. Display the contents of the file on the Browse screen. It is wider than the screen, so use the *Lock fields on left* command on the Fields menu to lock the first two fields on the screen. Then, use the keys described in Table 13 to scroll the screen horizontally.

Use the Forward or Backward search commands on the Go To menu to search the fields that contain the data listed in the grid below. List the states that contain that data in the spaces provided. (Table 12 describes the fields in the database.)

Field	Data	State
POP01080	401851	
PCI01079	6380	
PCI11085	23	
POP13086	5	

▼QUESTIONS

1. Why might you want to display specific records?
2. What is a record pointer?
3. List and briefly describe the two screens that you can display records on. How do they differ?
4. List the steps you follow to use the search command.
5. What wildcards can you use in the search command? Describe them.

▼ CONCEPTS

Besides death and taxes there is at least one other certainty in life. The sooner you collect all the information you need, the sooner it will be outdated and require modifications to keep it up to date. With card files, this is quite straightforward. All you have to do is read through a card file until you find the card that is in error, and then replace it with a corrected card. Though straightforward, finding the card is not necessarily fast. Think of the problem of updating a card file with 500 cards in it, even if they are in alphabetical order. To update the file, you would have to sort through all 500 cards each time you wanted to find the one to update. A database management program lets you update your records much more easily. You just find the record, then edit information in its fields, or even add or delete complete records.

You can update records on either the Edit or Browse screen. You navigate these screens with the commands described in Table 13 and edit records with those described in Table 14. Other commands you can use are discussed below.

ADDING RECORDS

When you want to add new records to a file, you open the database file, and then display the Edit or Browse screen. You then move the highlight to the end of the file and type in the new record's data, just as you entered the initial records into the file. Unlike a card index file, where you would want to insert the card into the proper order, the program adds it to the end of the file (Figure 25). New records can be added one after another without worrying about the order they are added in. After they have been entered, they can be easily sorted into any desired order.

ID	LASTNAME	FIRST	STREET	CITY	ST	ZIP	AREA	PHONE	
101	Culman	Tina	100 Elm Street	New Haven	CT	10000	203	555-1000	
102	Benjamin	Nancy	25 Oak Street	Cambridge	MA	20000	617	555-1001	
103	Kendall	Liz	14 Lark Ave.	Chicago	IL	20000	312	555-1002	
104	Hogan	Dennis	40 Main Street	Edgewater	NJ	30000	201	555-1003	
105	Swabey	Daphne	168 Bridge Road	Beverly	MA	20000	617	555-1004	
106	Sobel	Carol	45 Porter Ave.	Fairlawn	NJ	30000	201	555-1005	
107	Anthony	William	900 Maple Road	Reading	MA	20000	617	555-1006	
108	Poe	James	10 Preston Lane	Oakland	CA	40000	415	555-1007	
109	Fiske	Robert	1500 Storybrook	Boston	MA	02098	617	555-1008	
110	Porsena	Lars	110 Millbrook	Austin	TX	50000	512	555-1009	
111	Alverez	Jose	25 Stuart Road	Miami	FL	60000	305	555-1010	
112	Davis	John	26 Alpine Road	Elmherst	IL	50000	312	555-1020	← Added Record

FIGURE 25   Adding Records.   When you add records, they are added at the end of the file.

UPDATING RECORDS

It is often necessary to update records in a database file; for example, when customers change addresses, their records must be updated. To do this, you first use the command to find the specific record to be updated and display it on the screen. You then revise the contents of the appropriate fields. Revised records are saved automatically when you move the highlight to a new record after editing them. There are five menu options that you can use when updating your records:

- The *Blank record* choice on the Records menu deletes all data in a record but leaves the record in the database so that you can enter new data.
- The *Undo change to record* choice on the Records menu undoes changes made to the current record if you select it before moving the cursor to a new record or press F2 to change screens. After changes are saved they cannot be automatically undone with this command.
- The *Blank field* choice on the Fields menu (Browse screen only) blanks the field containing the highlight. (You can also blank the field by pressing CTRL-Y when the cursor is under the first character.)
- The *Freeze field* choice on the Fields menu (Browse screen only) freezes the highlight in the specified field so that you can enter or change data in that field in a number of records. After entering or editing data, press Enter to move the highlight to the same field in the next record.
- The *Size field* choice on the Fields menu (Browse screen only) changes the field's width on the screen (but not in the database file itself) so that you can narrow fields to see more on the screen at one time. The sizes automatically return to normal the next time you display the file on the Browse or Edit screen.

DELETING RECORDS

If a customer no longer buys from the company, a product is no longer manufactured, or an item is no longer in inventory, its record in a database file is no longer needed. These unwanted records should be deleted from the file. To do this, you first use the command to find the specific record to be deleted and display it on the screen. You then mark the record for deletion. The deleted record is just marked with an electronic flag. You can choose whether marked files are included in other operations or if they are hidden (see ''TIPS'' below). The marked records can be permanently removed by an operation called packing.

▼PROCEDURES

This section describes the procedures that you follow to:

- Add records
- Update records
- Mark and unmark records for deletion
- Remove marked records from the database

To Add Records to a Database

1. Highlight the database on the Control Center's Data panel, and then press F2 to display its data. (Press F2 to select the Edit or Browse screen.)
2. Either press ALT-G to pull down the Go To menu, and then press L for *Last record*. Press PGDN (Edit screen) or ↓ (Browse screen), and the prompt reads ===> *Add new records? (Y/N)*. Press Y to display a blank record.

   Or press ALT-R to pull down the Records menu, and then press A for *Add new records.*
3. Enter records just as you did when you first created the database.
4. When you are finished, press ALT-E to pull down the Exit menu, and then press E for *Exit.*

To Update Records in a Database

1. Highlight the database on the Control Center's Data panel, and then press F2 to display its data. (You can press F2 to switch between the Edit or Browse screen.)
2. Use the commands described in Table 13 to move the highlight to the record and field that you want to revise.
3. Type the new data in the fields, and use the editing commands described in Table 14.
4. When you are finished, press ALT-E to pull down the Exit menu, and then press E for *Exit.*

To Mark or Unmark Individual Records for Deletion

1. Highlight the database on the Control Center's Data panel, and then press F2 to display its data. (You can press F2 to switch between Edit and Browse modes.)
2. Move the highlight to any field in the record that you want to mark or unmark for deletion. (When the highlight is positioned in any field of a record marked for deletion, the right end of the status bar displays *Del.)*
3. Either press CTRL-U to mark or unmark the record.
   Or   press ALT-R to pull down the Records menu, and then press M for *Mark record for deletion* or C for *Clear deletion mark.*
4. Press ALT-E to pull down the Exit menu, then press E for *Exit* to return to the Control Center.

To Detete Marked Records or Remove all Marks

1. Highlight the name of the database in the Control Center's Data panel.
2. Press SHIFT-F2 to display the database design screen, and the Organize menu is automatically pulled down.
3. Either press E for *Erase marked records,* and the prompt reads *Are you sure you want to erase marked records?.* Press Y.
   Or   press U for *Unmark all files,* and the prompt reads *Are you sure you want to unmark all records marked for deletion?.* Press Y.
4. Press ALT-E to pull down the Exit menu, and then press E for *Exit* to return to the Control Center.

▼ TIPS

➤ **You can specify if records marked for deletion are displayed or not.** To do so from the Control Center, press ALT-T to pull down the Tools menu, and then press S for *Settings.* Move the highlight to the *Delete* option, and then press SPACEBAR to switch the setting between *ON* and *OFF.* (When set to *ON,* marked records are ignored.) Press ALT-E to pull down the Exit menu, and then press E for *Exit to Control Center.*

➤ **After marking records for deletion, you can preview those records.** Open the file with the marked records, highlight ⟨create⟩ on the Control Center's Queries panel, and then press ENTER to display the queries design screen. Press ALT-C to pull down the Condition menu, and then press A for *Add deletion box.* Type the function **DELETED( )** and then press F2 to process the query. The Browse screen is displayed listing all records marked for deletion. Unmark any files you do not want deleted. Press ALT-E to pull down the Exit menu, and then press E for *Exit.* The prompt reads *Query* *design has been changed. Do you want to save it?.* Press N to return to the Control Center.

➤ **The Lock record choice on the Browse and Edit screens' Records menu** is used on networks to lock a record you are working on. When locked, no one else can change data while your cursor is in the record. When you move the cursor from the record, it is unlocked. (You can also lock the current record by pressing CTRL-O.)

TUTORIAL 7A
Updating the NAMELIST File

In this tutorial, you add, update, and delete records in the NAMELIST file.

Step 1 **Open the NAMELIST File.** Before proceeding:

1. Load dBASE so that the Control Center is displayed.
2. Insert your data disk into drive A, and then change the default drive to drive A. (The current file and description section of the Control Center should read *A:\MYFILES.CAT.*)
3. Open the NAMELIST database so that its name is above the ruled line in the Control Center's Data panel.

Step 2 **Add a Record on the Edit Screen.** In Topic 5, you entered records into the database file. You can use the same commands to add new records to the end of the file. Here, you add a record using the Edit screen.

To add a record on the Edit screen

Press   F2 to display the Edit screen. (If the Browse screen is displayed, press F2 again.)

Press   ALT-R to pull down the Records menu

Press   A for *Add new records*

Result. A blank record appears. Enter the record shown in Table 16. If the data you enter does not fill a field, press ENTER to move the cursor to the next field. When you enter the last field of the record, a new blank record is displayed. When you are finished, press PGUP to return to the record you just added. Check it against Table 16.

Step 3 **Add Records on the Browse Screen.** Now use the Browse screen to enter new records.

To add records on Browse screen

Press   F2 to display the Browse screen

Press   ↓ to move the highlight to the last record

Press   ↓ one more time, and the prompt reads *Add new records? (Y/N)*

Press   Y to display a blank record

TABLE 16   Record to Add to the NAMELIST File on Edit Screen

Field	Data
ID:	109
LASTNAME:	Fiske
FIRST:	Robert
STREET:	1500 Storybrook
CITY:	Boston
ST:	MA
ZIP:	02098
AREA:	617
PHONE:	555-1008

Result. A new blank record is displayed on the screen. Enter the two records shown in Table 17. If the data you enter does not fill a field, press ENTER to move the cursor to the next field. When you enter the last field of the last record, the highlight moves down to the next blank record. Press ↑ to return to the last record you just added. Check the new records against Table 17.

TABLE 17   Records to Add to the NAMELIST File on Browse Screen

Field	Data	Field	Data
First Record		*Second Record*	
ID:	**110**	ID:	**111**
LASTNAME:	**Porsena**	LASTNAME:	**Alverez**
FIRST:	**Lars**	FIRST:	**Jose**
STREET:	**110 Millbrook**	STREET:	**25 Stuart Road**
CITY:	**Austin**	CITY:	**Miami**
ST:	**TX**	ST:	**FL**
ZIP:	**50000**	ZIP:	**60000**
AREA:	**512**	AREA:	**305**
PHONE:	**555-1009**	PHONE:	**555-1010**

Step 4   **Edit a Record.** To edit a record, you simply display the record, and then you edit it. Here you change an address and phone number for someone who has moved. Before proceeding, display the Edit screen.

To find the Kendall record

Press	TAB to move the cursor to the *LASTNAME* field
Press	ALT-G to pull down the Go To menu
Press	T for *Top record*
Press	ALT-G to pull down the Go To menu
Press	F for *Forward search*, and the prompt reads *Enter search string*
Type	**Kendall** and then press ENTER

To change Kendall's address and phone number

Press	TAB to move the cursor to the *STREET* field
Press	CTRL-Y to delete the field's contents
Type	**26 Rosewood** and then press TAB to move to the *PHONE* field
Press	CTRL-Y to delete the field's contents
Type	**556-1200** and then the next record is displayed
Press	PGUP to return to the record you edited, and then check it

Result. The record should look like the one in Figure 26.

Step 5   **Mark a Record for Deletion.** When records are no longer needed, you can delete them from the file. This is a two-step process: First you mark them, and then you delete them. Before proceeding, display the Browse screen.

To mark a record for deletion

Move	the highlight to record 8 (ID number 108)
Press	CTRL-U

Result. The status bar reads *Del.* Press CTRL-U a few more times. Each time you press it you mark or unmark the record. When you are finished, be sure the status bar reads *Del.*

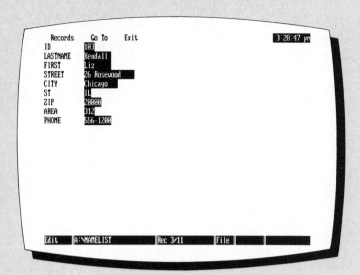

FIGURE 26 The Updated Record.
After revising the record, it should look like this.

Step 6 **Delete the Marked Record.** Now, permanently delete the record.

To return to the Control Center

Press   ALT-E to pull down the Exit menu, and then press E for *Exit*

To delete the marked record

Highlight   *NAMELIST* on the Control Center's Data panel

Press   SHIFT-F2 to display the database design screen, and the Organize menu is automatically pulled down

Press   E for *Erase marked records,* and the prompt reads *Are you sure you want to erase marked records?*

Press   Y and a message box keeps you posted on the process

Press   ALT-E to pull down the Exit menu, and then press S for *Save changes and exit*

Result.   The Control Center reappears.

Step 7 **Display the Remaining Files.** To confirm that the record has been deleted, display the data in the file.

To display the data

Highlight   *NAMELIST,* and then press F2. (If the Browse screen is not displayed, press F2 again.)

Result.   Press PGUP to display all records. The record for ID 108 is no longer listed. Press ALT-E to pull down the Exit menu, and then press E for *Exit* to return to the Control Center.

Step 8 **Print Out the Records.** Make a printout of the records in the database file. Before proceeding, be sure that the printer is ready.

To print out the records

Press   SHIFT-F9 to display a submenu

Press   B for *Begin printing*

Result.   The records are printed out.

Step 9 **Continue or Quit.** You have now completed this tutorial. Either continue with the next tutorial or quit the program.

TUTORIAL 7B
Updating the AMOUNTS File

In this tutorial, you add, update, and delete records in the AMOUNTS file.

Step 1   **Open the AMOUNTS File.** Before proceeding:

1. Load dBASE so that the Control Center is displayed.
2. Insert your data disk into drive A, and then change the default drive to drive A. (The current file and description section of the Control Center should read *A:\MYFILES.CAT.*)
3. Open the AMOUNTS database so that its name is above the ruled line in the Control Center's Data panel.

Step 2   **Edit a Record.** You can edit a specific record. Before proceeding, display the Edit screen.

To go to record number 5

Press   ALT-G to pull down the Go To menu

Press   R for *Record number,* and the prompt reads *Enter record number:*

Type   **5** and then press ENTER

To edit a file

Move   the highlight to the *AMOUNT* field

Press   CTRL-Y to delete the field's contents

Type   **30.00** and then the next record is displayed

Result.   The next record is automatically displayed. Press PGUP to return to the record you updated.

Step 3   **Add a Record on the Edit Screen.** Here, you add a record on the Edit screen.

To add a record on the Edit screen

Press   ALT-R to pull down the Records menu

Press   A for *Add new records*

Result.   A blank record appears. Enter the record shown in Table 18. If the data you enter does not fill a field, press ENTER to move the cursor to the next field. When you enter the last field of the record, a new blank record is displayed. When you are finished, press PGUP to return to the record you just added. Check it against Table 18.

TABLE 18   Record to Add to the AMOUNTS File on Edit Screen

Field	Data
ID:	109
DATE:	06/16/90
AMOUNT:	18.00

Step 4   **Add Records on the Browse Screen.** Now use the Browse screen to enter new records.

**TABLE 19   Records to Add to the AMOUNTS File
on Browse Screen**

Field	Data	Field	Data
First Record		*Second Record*	
ID:	**110**	*ID:*	**111**
DATE:	**06/17/90**	*DATE:*	**06/18/90**
AMOUNT:	**43.00**	*AMOUNT:*	**61.00**

To add records on the Browse screen

Press	F2 to display the Browse screen
Highlight	the last record
Press	↓ one more time, and the prompt reads *Add new records?* *(Y/N)*
Press	Y to display a blank record

Result. A new blank record is displayed on the screen. Enter the two records shown in Table 19. If the data you enter does not fill a field, press ENTER to move the cursor to the next field. When you enter the last field of the last record, the highlight moves down to the next blank record. Press ↑ to return to the last record you just added. Check the new records against Table 19.

Step 5 Mark a Record for Deletion. When records are no longer needed, you can delete them from the file. This is a two-step process: First you mark them, and then you delete them. Before proceeding, display the Browse screen.

To mark a record for deletion

Move	the highlight to record 8 (ID number 108)
Press	CTRL-U

Result. The status bar reads *Del.* Press CTRL-U a few more times. Each time you press it you mark or unmark the record. When you are finished, be sure the status bar reads *Del.*

Step 6 Delete the Marked Record. Now, permanently delete the record.

To return to the Control Center

Press	ALT-E to pull down the Exit menu
Press	E for *Exit*

To delete the marked record

Highlight	*AMOUNTS* on the Control Center's Data panel
Press	SHIFT-F2 to display the database design screen, and the Organize menu is automatically pulled down
Press	E for *Erase marked records,* and the prompt reads *Are you sure you want to erase marked records?*
Press	Y and a message box keeps you posted on the process
Press	ALT-E to pull down the Exit menu, and then press S for *Save changes and exit*

Result. The Control Center reappears.

Step 7 Display the Remaining Files. To confirm that the record has been deleted, display the data in the file.

To display the data

Press	F2 (If the Browse screen is not displayed, press F2 again.)

Result. Press PGUP to display all records. The record for ID 108 is no longer listed. Press ALT-E to pull down the Exit menu, and then press E for *Exit* to return to the Control Center.

Step 8 **Print Out the Records.** Make a printout of the records in the database file. Before proceeding, be sure that the printer is ready.

To print out the records
Press   SHIFT-F9 to display a submenu
Press   B for *Begin printing*

Result. The records are printed out.

Step 9 **Continue or Quit.** You have now completed this tutorial. Either continue with the next tutorial or quit the program.

▼EXERCISE

EXERCISE 7A   Add and Delete Records from the COURSES File

Open the COURSES file that you entered records into in Exercise 5A. Add your own courses to the database. Mark the US History course for deletion, and then remove it from the file. Print a quick report of the changes.

▼QUESTIONS

1. When you add new records to a file, where are they stored in the file?
2. When editing a record, what command can you use to delete the information in a field? In all fields in the record?
3. When you delete a record, what does the program do before permanently deleting the record? How do you permanently delete records?

▼ CONCEPTS

Sorting a file rearranges the records into a specified order and saves them to a new file on the disk (Figure 27). To sort a file, you first determine what information is to be arranged in order. For example, you can sort the file so that the names are arranged alphabetically, or you can sort it so that a given set of numbers is arranged in ascending or descending order. Since these values are stored in fields, you actually specify what field is to be reordered and in what order its data are to be sorted. When the file is sorted based on a specific field, all the records are rearranged, not just the fields. When you specify which field is to be used, you are designating it as the key. You can often specify more than one key—one primary key and one or more secondary keys.

The primary key is the field that is sorted first. If you are sorting a list of names in the original file, the primary key will sort it so that all the names are in ascending or descending alphabetical order. Ideally, a primary key contains unique information, for example, a driver's license number, an employee number, or a social security number.

Sometimes a unique field does not exist or serve your purpose. For example, when you sort a file by last names the file may have more than one person with the same last name. In these cases, a perfect sort is not achieved using just a primary key; a secondary key, like the first name, must be used to break ties. If you want to sort on more than one field, you select each field in turn, and specify if it is to be sorted in ascending or descending order.

FIGURE 27   Sorting a File.   When you sort a file, you specify the fields it is to be sorted on and the order of the sort. The original file (a) is then written to a new file in the specified order (b).

#	LASTNAME	FIRSTNAME
1	Smith	Vance
2	Jones	Marie
3	Lewis	John
4	Jones	Stuart
5	Curtin	Dennis
6	Smith	Adam
7	Stanford	David
8	Smith	Robert
9	Benjamin	Nancy
10	Swabey	Daphne
11	Vogel	Terry
12	Smith	Frank
13	Jones	Lewis

A. Original Unsorted File

#	LASTNAME	FIRSTNAME
9	Benjamin	Nancy
5	Curtin	Dennis
13	Jones	Lewis
2	Jones	Marie
4	Jones	Stuart
3	Lewis	John
6	Smith	Adam
12	Smith	Frank
8	Smith	Robert
1	Smith	Vance
7	Stanford	David
10	Swabey	Daphne
11	Vogel	Terry

B. New File Sorted by LASTNAME in Ascending Order

▼ PROCEDURES

This section describes the procedures that you follow to:

• Sort a database file to a new file on the disk

To Sort to a New File on the Disk

1. Open the database file that you want to sort.
2. Press SHIFT-F2 to display the database design screen, and the Organize menu is automatically pulled down.
3. Press S for *Sort database on field list* to display a box. The cursor is in the *Field order* column.
4. Press SHIFT-F1 to display a list of fields to choose from, highlight the one you want, and then press ENTER.
5. Press TAB to move the highlight to the *Type of sort* column, and then press SPACEBAR to cycle through the four options. (See Table 20 for a list of the options and Table 21 for an example of how each sorts a file.)
6. If you want to sort on more than one field, press ↓ and then repeat Steps 4 and 5.)
7. Press CTRL-END to save the settings, and the prompt reads *Enter name of sorted file.*
8. Type the name of the file you want the sorted records stored in, and then press ENTER.
9. Press ALT-E to pull down the Exit menu, and then press S for *Save changes and exit* to return to the Control Center. The new file is listed in the Data panel.

TABLE 20   Sort Options

Option	Description
Ascending ASCII	A..Z a..z 0..9
Descending ASCII	z..a Z..A 9..0
Ascending Dictionary	Aa..Zz 0..9
Descending Dictionary	zZ..aA 9..0

TABLE 21   Sort Orders

A..Z a..z	z..a Z..A	Aa..Zz	zZ..aA
Aardvark	zebra	Aardvark	zebra
Zebra	aardvark	aardvark	Zebra
aardvark	Zebra	Zebra	aardvark
zebra	aardvark	zebra	Aardvark

TUTORIAL 8A
Sorting the NAMELIST File to a Separate File

In this tutorial, you sort the NAMELIST file.

Step 1 **Open the NAMELIST File.** Before proceeding:

1. Load dBASE so that the Control Center is displayed.
2. Insert your data disk into drive A, and then change the default drive to drive A. (The current file and description section of the Control Center should read *A:\MYFILES.CAT.*)
3. Open the NAMELIST database so that its name is above the ruled line in the Control Center's Data panel.

Step 2 **Sort the NAMELIST File.** Now, let's sort the NAMELIST file to a file named NAMESORT. When you do so, you will sort the file on two fields, LASTNAME and FIRST. LASTNAME is the primary key, so it will be listed first.

To sort the file

Press	SHIFT-F2 to display the database design screen, and the Organize menu is automatically pulled down
Press	S for *Sort database on field list* to display a box. The cursor is in the *Field order* column
Press	SHIFT-F1 to display a list to choose from, highlight *LASTNAME,* and then press ENTER
Press	TAB to move the highlight to the *Type of sort* column, and then press SPACEBAR to cycle to the option *Ascending ASCII* (If you go past it, press SPACEBAR until it appears again.)
Press	↓ to move the highlight down one field
Press	SHIFT-F1 to display a list to choose from, highlight *FIRST,* and then press ENTER
Press	TAB to move the highlight to the *Type of sort* column, and then press SPACEBAR to cycle to the option *Ascending ASCII* (If you go past it, press SPACEBAR until it appears again.)
Press	CTRL-END to save the settings, and the prompt reads *Enter name of sorted file:*
Type	**NAMESORT** and then press ENTER
Press	ALT-E to pull down the Exit menu, and then press S for *Save changes and exit* to return to the Control Center

Result. The new file is listed in the Data panel. Highlight its name, and then press F2 to display the file's contents. The new file is sorted by last name in ascending order. Press ALT-E to pull down the Exit menu, and then press E for *Exit* to return to the Control Center.

Step 3 **Print the Sorted File.** Make a printout of the records in the database file. Before proceeding, be sure that the printer is ready.

To print out the records

Press	SHIFT-F9 to display a submenu
Press	B for *Begin printing*

Result. The records are printed out. Compare the results with a previous printout that you made of the unsorted NAMELIST file.

Step 4 **Continue or Quit.** You have now completed this tutorial. Either continue with the next tutorial or quit the program.

TUTORIAL 8B
Sorting the AMOUNTS File to a Separate File

In this tutorial, you sort the AMOUNTS file.

Step 1 **Open the AMOUNTS File.** Before proceeding:

1. Load dBASE so that the Control Center is displayed.
2. Insert your data disk into drive A, and then change the default drive to drive A. (The current file and description section of the Control Center should read *A:\MYFILES.CAT.*)
3. Open the AMOUNTS database so that its name is above the ruled line in the Control Center's Data panel.

Step 2 **Sort the AMOUNTS File.** Now, let's sort the AMOUNTS file to a file named AMTSORT.

To sort the file

Press   SHIFT-F2 to display the database design screen, and the Organize menu is automatically pulled down

Press   S for *Sort database on field list* to display a box. The cursor is in the *Field order* column

Press   SHIFT-F1 to display a list to choose from, highlight *AMOUNT,* and then press ENTER

Press   TAB to move the highlight to the Type of sort column, and then press SPACEBAR to cycle to the option *Descending ASCII* (If you go past it, press SPACEBAR until it appears again.)

Press   CTRL-END to save the settings, and the prompt reads *Enter name of sorted file:*

Type   **AMTSORT** and then press ENTER

Press   ALT-E to pull down the Exit menu, and then press S for *Save changes and exit* to return to the Control Center

Result. The new file is listed in the Data panel. Highlight its name, and then press F2 to display the file's contents. The new file is sorted by amount in descending order. Press ALT-E to pull down the Exit menu, and then press E for *Exit* to return to the Control Center.

Step 3 **Print the Sorted File.** Make a printout of the records in the database file. Before proceeding, be sure that the printer is ready.

To print out the records

Press   SHIFT-F9 to display a submenu

Press   B for *Begin printing*

Result. The records are printed out. Compare the results with a previous printout that you made of the unsorted AMOUNTS file.

Step 4 **Continue or Quit.** You have now completed this tutorial. Either continue with the next tutorial or quit the program.

▼EXERCISES

EXERCISE 8A   Sort the COURSES File

Open the COURSES database, and then sort it in descending order using the field you enter course numbers into. Sort it to a file named COURSES2 and then print a quick report of that file.

EXERCISE 8B   Sort the PLACEST File

Open the PLACEST database, and then sort it on the POP13086 field (Population percent change 1980-1986) in ascending order. Sort it to a file named PLACEST2 and then print a quick report of that file. Which state had the largest population increase in the period? The largest decrease? Table 12 describes the fields in the report.

Add a description to the file indicating that it is sorted by "Population percent change 1980-1986."

▼QUESTIONS

1. Why might you want to sort a file?
2. Explain the purpose of a key field.
3. What is the purpose of a primary key? A secondary key?
4. What is a tie in a sort?
5. Into what orders can you sort a file?
6. How do you specify that you want to sort the file on more than one field?

TOPIC 9
Indexing Files

▼**CONCEPTS**

Sorting is not always the best way to arrange a file.

- It can take a long time to sort an entire file if the database contains a lot of records.
- A file can be sorted in only one order at a time. For example, a name and address file used for mailings might be sorted by last name to produce a reference list. It would then be sorted by ZIP code for printing mailing labels because the post office gives reduced rates for mailings that are presorted by ZIP code. To maintain lists like these in more than one order, you would need separate files, each sorted differently.
- Some commands, like *Index key search* on the Go To menu, work only on indexed fields. Searching the entire database for a string would take a very long time. Searching for the string in the index, and then displaying the matching record, is much faster.

To understand the difference between sorting and indexing, let's look at how a database management program finds a specific record without, and then with, an index.

SEQUENTIAL FILES

Records are physically stored in a file on the disk much like pages are organized in a book. When you search a sequential file for a specific record, the program begins at the beginning of the file and reads each record until it finds the one you want. If you create a file with many records, the data cannot all fit in the computer's memory at the same time. Much of it will be stored on one or more disks and read into memory as needed. When the program tries to sequentially find a file, it begins to read these records into memory in batches, looking for the record it wants. If it does not find the record, it replaces the first batch of records in memory with others from the disk and continues to look. Retrieving data from disks is slow compared to the speed of processing the records once they are in memory. It can take a long time just to find a specific record. If the program is also sorting the file into a specific order, it can go on for hours rearranging the records a few at a time.

Suppose your file has 10,000 records in it, and you want to find a specific record. Sequentially finding this record would be time consuming, especially if it were near the end of the file. On average, the program would have to read half the file, 5,000 records, before it found the record you wanted. Sequential file scans are fine if you always need to look at or process all the records in a file. But if you want to find only specific records, this method may be unsatisfactory. The solution to this problem is to index the file.

INDEXED FILES

The idea behind an indexed file is similar to that of an index at the back of a book. The index lets you look up a term and go directly to the page where it is discussed.

This is called direct access. Then you can sequentially search from there to find the exact place on the page. This combination of direct access and sequential search is called the index-sequential method.

To index a file, you specify the field you want it indexed by. Ideally, this field contains unique values. Once you specify the field, the program creates a shorter companion file for the index. The index contains only two things: the record number that the program assigned when you entered it and the contents of the indexed field (Figure 28). The field contents are sorted into ascending or descending order.

When you use an index to find a particular record, you specify the value to be looked for in the indexed field. The program first reads the index file and scans the records there. Since the index is generally much smaller than the file, this can be done quickly. When it finds a record that matches the search criteria you entered, it looks for its record number, or record pointer, and goes directly to where that record is stored on the disk. The computer then starts reading data records from that point until it finds the record it is looking for or one that has a higher key. If it finds a higher key, it knows the record it is looking for does not exist.

Indexes allow you to keep a file in order by several primary keys without having to physically resort it each time or maintain duplicate files. For example, the original file can have two indexes, one sorting it by department and another by phone number. You can also index a file on more than one field (called a complex index). This is similar to sorting a file using a primary and secondary key. To specify more than one field for the index, you connect the field names with plus (+) signs.

Once you have created an index, dBASE IV automatically maintains it. If you add, insert, or delete records in the file, the index is automatically updated, and the records are moved into the position specified by the index. For example, when you add a record to an indexed file, the new record changes position automatically when you move the cursor to another record if the *Follow record to new position* choice on the Browse screen's Record menu is set to *YES*. If set to *NO*, they don't change position. The same thing happens if you revise the field that the file is currently indexed on.

FIGURE 28 An Indexed File. Here, a database file (a) has been indexed by LASTNAME (b). The file remains in its original order, but the index is arranged alphabetically by last name. When searching for a record, the program searches the index file and then uses the record pointer to find the matching record in the database. These pointers give the physical location of where the records are stored in the file on the disk.

ID	LASTNAME	FIRST	STREET	CITY	ST	ZIP	AREA	PHONE
101	Culman	Tina	100 Elm Street	New Haven	CT	10000	203	555-1000
102	Benjamin	Nancy	25 Oak Street	Cambridge	MA	20000	617	555-1001
103	Kendall	Liz	14 Lark Ave.	Chicago	IL	20000	312	555-1002
104	Hogan	Dennis	40 Main Street	Edgewater	NJ	30000	201	555-1003
105	Swabey	Daphne	168 Bridge Road	Beverly	MA	20000	617	555-1004
106	Sobel	Carol	45 Porter Ave.	Fairlawn	NJ	30000	201	555-1005
107	Anthony	William	900 Maple Road	Reading	MA	20000	617	555-1006
108	Poe	James	10 Preston Lane	Oakland	CA	40000	415	555-1007
109	Fiske	Robert	1500 Storybrook	Boston	MA	02098	617	555-1008
110	Porsena	Lars	110 Millbrook	Austin	TX	50000	512	555-1009
111	Alverez	Jose	25 Stuart Road	Miami	FL	60000	305	555-1010
112	Davis	John	26 Alpine Road	Elmherst	IL	50000	312	555-1020

ID	LASTNAME
111	Alverez
107	Anthony
102	Benjamin
101	Culman
112	Davis
109	Fiske
104	Hogan
103	Kendall
108	Poe
110	Porsena
106	Sobel
105	Swabey

A. The Database File

B. The Index

How Indexes Are Stored

When you create an index, it is stored in a file with the same name as the database but with the extension .MDX. If you create more than one index for a file, they are stored together in this file. The file can contain up to 47 uniquely named indexes. You can specify which of the indexes to use (called the current index) by pressing SHIFT-F2 to display the database design screen and then selecting *Order records by index* from the Layout menu. This displays a list of the available indexes. To select one, you highlight it, and then press ENTER.

WORKING WITH INDEXED FILES

Once you have indexed a file, additional procedures become available to you.

The *Forward search* and *Backward search* commands on the Go To menu are quite slow when you use them with large databases. However, once you have indexed a file, you can use the *Index key search* choice to quickly search any indexed field. The command finds only the first occurrence, but since the file is indexed, all the related records follow immediately. When you enter the search string, keep the following points in mind:

- The search is case sensitive. You must enter the search string exactly as it appears in the file.
- The search looks for a match beginning at the first character in the field. If you search for ''Ken,'' you would move to the first record that contains those characters as the first characters in the field. Because the program searches beginning at the first character in the field, you don't have to enter the entire string—just enough characters to uniquely identify it.
- You cannot use wildcards.

▼PROCEDURES

This section describes the procedures that you follow to:

- Index a file
- Specify the current index for a file
- Use an index key search
- To index a file

To Index a File

1. Open the database file that you want to index.
2. Press SHIFT-F2 to display the database design screen, and the Organize menu is automatically pulled down.
3. Press C for *Create new index* to display a submenu.
4. Move the highlight to each of the menu choices described in Table 22, and then press ENTER. Enter the appropriate information, and then press ENTER again.
5. Press CTRL-END to save the index settings.
6. Press ALT-E to pull down the Exit menu, and then press S for *Save changes and exit*.

TABLE 22   Index Menu Choices

Choice	Description
Name of index	The name of the index, up to ten characters long, and following the same rules as field names (see Table 6 in Topic 4).
Index expression	The name of the field(s) to be indexed. If you specify more than one, connect them with plus (+) signs. The expression cannot contain the names of logical or memo fields. You can press SHIFT-F1 to display a list of field names from which to choose. After highlighting one, you can press ENTER twice to move to the next setting, or type + and then press SHIFT-F1 to select another field.
Order of index	Selects ascending or descending order.
Display first duplicate key only	Determines if two or more records with the same information in the indexed fields are displayed.

To Specify the Current Index for a File

1. Open the database file that you want to index.
2. Press SHIFT-F2 to display the database design screen, and the Organize menu is automatically pulled down.
3. Press O for *Order records by index* to display a list of indexes.
4. Highlight the desired index, and then press ENTER.
5. Press ALT-E to pull down the Exit menu, and then press E for *Exit* to return to the Control Center.
6. Press F2 to display the database arranged by the index.
7. Press ALT-E to pull down the Exit menu, and then press E for *Exit* to return to the Control Center.

Use an Index Key Search

1. Index the file on the field you want to search, and then display the Browse screen.
2. Press ALT-G to pull down the Go To menu.
3. Press I for *Index key search,* and the prompt reads *Enter search string for* followed by the index field's name.
4. Type the search string (or enough characters to uniquely identify it), and then press ENTER.

▼TIP

➤ **You can also index a file when you define it** by setting the *Index* attribute on the database design screen to *Y* for each field you want to create an index for. The indexes are then automatically generated and are assigned the names of the fields that you changed to *Y*.

TUTORIAL 9A
Indexing the NAMELIST File

In this tutorial, you index the NAMELIST.

Step 1   **Open the NAMELIST File.** Before proceeding:
1. Load dBASE so that the Control Center is displayed.
2. Insert your data disk into drive A, and then change the default drive to drive A. (The current file and description section of the Control Center should read *A:\MYFILES.CAT*.)
3. Open the NAMELIST database so that its name is above the ruled line in the Control Center's Data panel.

Step 2   **Index the File.** First, create a new index, and then use it to order the file.

To create an index on the LASTNAME field

Press	SHIFT-F2 to display the database design screen, and the Organize menu is automatically pulled down
Press	C for *Create new index* to display a submenu
Press	N for *Name of index*, type **LAST** and then press ENTER
Press	I for *Index expression*
Press	SHIFT-F1 to display a list of field names, highlight *LASTNAME*, and then press ENTER twice
Press	O for *Order of index*. Each time you press it the setting changes between *ASCENDING* and *DESCENDING*. Set it to *ASCENDING*
Press	CTRL-END to index the file and display a message indicating the progress
Press	F2 to display the file arranged by the index

Result.   The file now appears sorted by last name in ascending order although the records in the file have not been physically sorted.

Step 3   **Create Another Index.** One advantage of indexes is that a file can be kept in more than one order. To do this, you create additional indexes. Let's create a new index based on the ST field and then look at the file using this new index and the LAST index created previously.

To create an index on the ST field

Press	ALT-E to pull down the Exit menu
Press	R for *Return to database design*, and the Organize menu is automatically pulled down
Press	C for *Create new index* to display a submenu
Press	N for *Name of index*, type **ST**, and then press ENTER
Press	I for *Index expression*
Press	SHIFT-F1 to display a list of field names, highlight *ST*, and then press ENTER twice
Press	O for *Order of index*, and then set it to *ASCENDING*
Press	CTRL-END to index the file and display a message indicating the progress
Press	F2 to display the file arranged by the index

Result.   The file now appears sorted by state in ascending order.

Step 4   **Index on Multiple Fields.** Instead of creating indexes on a single field, you can specify more than one field to create a complex index.

To index multiple fields

Press	ALT-E to pull down the Exit menu
Press	R for *Return to database design,* and the Organize menu is automatically pulled down
Press	C for *Create new index* to display a submenu
Press	N for *Name of index,* type **STNAME**, and then press ENTER
Press	I for *Index expression*
Press	SHIFT-F1 to display a list of field names, highlight *ST,* and then press ENTER
Type	+ and the entry now reads *ST+*
Press	SHIFT-F1 to display a list of field names, highlight *LASTNAME,* and then press ENTER twice. The entry now reads *ST+LASTNAME*
Press	O for *Order of index,* and then set it to *DESCENDING*
Press	CTRL-END to index the file and display a message indicating the progress
Press	F2 to display the file arranged by the index

Result. The file now appears sorted first by state and then by last name in descending order.

Step 5 **Modify an Index.** After creating an index, you can modify it at any time. Let's modify the STNAME index to change the order to ascending.

To modify an index

Press	ALT-E to pull down the Exit menu
Press	R for *Return to database design,* and the Organize menu is automatically pulled down
Press	M for *Modify existing index* to display a list of available indexes
Highlight	STNAME, and then press ENTER
Press	O for *Order of index,* and then set it to *ASCENDING*
Press	CTRL-END to index the file and display a message indicating the progress
Press	F2 to display the file arranged by the index

Result. The file now appears sorted first by state and then by last name in ascending order.

Step 6 **Change the Index.** When you have more than one index, as you do here, you can specify which index is to be used.

To specify an index

Press	ALT-E to pull down the Exit menu
Press	R for *Return to database design,* and the Organize menu is automatically pulled down
Press	O for *Order records by index* to display a list of available indexes
Highlight	LAST, and then press ENTER
Press	F2 to display the file arranged by the index

Result. The file is now arranged using the LAST index.

Step 7 **Use Index Key Search.** Now that the file is indexed on the last name, let's use the *Index key search* command to find a record in that field. When you enter the string to search for, you only have to enter enough characters so the string can be uniquely identified. Here you enter ''Ken'' to find ''Kendall.''

To search an indexed field

Press   ALT-G to pull down the Go To menu

Press   I for *Index key search,* and the prompt reads *Enter search string for LASTNAME:*

Type   **Ken** and then press Enter

Result.   The cursor immediately jumps to the first record that has an entry with Kendall in the LASTNAME field. Press ALT-E to pull down the Exit menu, and then press E for *Exit* to return to the Control Center.

Step 8   **Continue or Quit.** You have now completed this tutorial. Either continue with the next tutorial or quit the program.

TUTORIAL 9B
Indexing the AMOUNTS File

In this tutorial, you index the AMOUNTS file.

Step 1   **Open the AMOUNTS File.** Before proceeding:

1. Load dBASE so that the Control Center is displayed.
2. Insert your data disk into drive A, and then change the default drive to drive A. (The current file and description section of the Control Center should read *A:\MYFILES.CAT.*)
3. Open the AMOUNTS database so that its name is above the ruled line in the Control Center's Data panel.

Step 2   **Index the File.** First, create a new index, and then use it to order the file.

To create an index on the AMOUNT field

Press   SHIFT-F2 to display the database design screen, and the Organize menu is automatically pulled down

Press   C for *Create new index* to display a submenu

Press   N for *Name of index,* type **AMOUNT** and then press ENTER

Press   I for *Index expression*

Press   SHIFT-F1 to display a list of field names, highlight *AMOUNT,* and then press ENTER twice

Press   O for *Order of index.* Each time you press it the setting changes between *ASCENDING* and *DESCENDING.* Set it to *ASCENDING*

Press   CTRL-END to index the file and display a message indicating the progress

Press   F2 to display the file arranged by the index

Result.   The file now appears sorted by amount in ascending order although the records in the file have not been physically sorted.

Step 3   **Create Another Index.** Let's create a new index based on the DATE field.

To create an index on the DATE field

Press	ALT-E to pull down the Exit menu
Press	R for *Return to database design,* and the Organize menu is automatically pulled down
Press	C for *Create new index* to display a submenu
Press	N for *Name of index,* type **DATE** and then press ENTER
Press	I for *Index expression*
Press	SHIFT-F1 to display a list of field names, highlight *DATE,* and then press ENTER twice
Press	O for *Order of index,* and then set it to *ASCENDING*
Press	CTRL-END to index the file and display a message indicating the progress
Press	F2 to display the file arranged by the index

Result.   The file now appears sorted by date in ascending order.

Step 4   **Index on Multiple Fields.** Instead of creating indexes on a single field, you can specify more than one field to create complex indexes.

To index multiple fields

Press	ALT-E to pull down the Exit menu
Press	R for *Return to database design*, and the Organize menu is automatically pulled down
Press	C for *Create new index* to display a submenu
Press	N for *Name of index,* type **AMTDATE** and then press ENTER
Press	I for *Index expression*
Press	SHIFT-F1 to display a list of field names, highlight *AMOUNT,* and then press ENTER
Type	+ and the entry now reads *AMOUNT+*
Press	SHIFT-F1 to display a list of field names, highlight *DATE,* and then press ENTER twice. The entry now reads *AMOUNT+DATE*
Press	O for *Order of index,* and then set it to *ASCENDING*
Press	CTRL-END to index the file and display a message indicating the progress
Press	F2 to display the file arranged by the index

Result.   The file now appears sorted first by amount and then by date.

Step 5   **Modify an Index.** After creating an index, you can modify it at any time. Let's modify the AMTDATE index to change the order to descending.

To modify an index

Press	ALT-E to pull down the Exit menu
Press	R for *Return to database design*, and the Organize menu is automatically pulled down
Press	M for *Modify existing index* to display a list of available indexes
Highlight	*AMTDATE,* and then press Enter
Press	O for *Order of index,* and then set it to *DESCENDING*
Press	CTRL-END to index the file and display a message indicating the progress
Press	F2 to display the file arranged by the index

Result.   The file now appears sorted first by state and then by last name in descending order.

Step 6   **Change the Index.** When you have more than one index, as you do here, you can specify which index is to be used.

To specify an index

Press	ALT-E to pull down the Exit menu
Press	R for *Return to database design*, and the Organize menu is automatically pulled down
Press	O for *Order records by index* to display a list of available indexes
Highlight	*AMOUNT*, and then press ENTER
Press	F2 to display the file arranged by the index

Result. The file is now arranged using the AMOUNT index. Press ALT-E to pull down the Exit menu, and then press E for *Exit* to return to the Control Center.

Step 7 Continue or Quit. You have now completed this tutorial. Either continue with the next tutorial or quit the program.

TUTORIAL 9C
Updating the Indexed NAMELIST File

In this tutorial, you add a record to the indexed NAMELIST file.

Step 1 Open the NAMELIST File. Before proceeding:

1. Load dBASE so that the Control Center is displayed.
2. Insert your data disk into drive A, and then change the default drive to drive A. (The current file and description section of the Control Center should read A:*MYFILES.CAT*.)
3. Open the NAMELIST database so that its name is above the ruled line in the Control Center's Data panel.

Step 2 Specify the Index. When you have more than one index, as you do here, you can specify which index is to be used.

To specify an index

Press	SHIFT-F2 to display the database design screen, and the Organize menu is automatically pulled down
Press	O for *Order records by index* to display a list of available indexes
Highlight	*LAST*, and then press ENTER
Press	F2 to display the file arranged by the index

Result. The file is now arranged using the LAST index.

Step 3 Add a Record. Now, add a new record to the indexed file.

To add a record on the Edit screen

Press	F2 (if necessary) to display the Edit screen
Press	ALT-R to pull down the Records menu
Press	A for *Add new records*

Result. A blank record appears. Enter the record shown in Table 23. After entering the last field, press ↑. The new record immediately moves to the position

89

TABLE 23   New Record Added to Indexed File

Field	Data
ID:	112
LASTNAME:	Davis
FIRST:	John
STREET:	26 Alpine Road
CITY:	Elmherst
ST:	IL
ZIP:	50000
AREA:	312
PHONE:	555-1020

position specified by the index. It appears in the correct position for the file indexed by last name. (You may have to press PgUp one or more times to see it.)

Step 4   **Print Out the Records.** Make a printout of the records in the database file. Before proceeding, be sure that the printer is ready.

To print out the records

Press   ALT-E to pull down the Exit menu, and then press E for *Exit* to return to the Control Center

Press   SHIFT-F9 to display a submenu

Press   B for *Begin printing*

Result.   The records are printed out.

Step 5   **Continue or Quit.** You have now completed this tutorial. Either continue with the next tutorial or quit the program.

TUTORIAL 9D
Updating the Indexed AMOUNTS File

In this tutorial, you update the indexed AMOUNTS file.

Step 1   **Open the AMOUNTS File.** Before proceeding:

1. Load dBASE so that the Control Center is displayed.
2. Insert your data disk into drive A, and then change the default drive to drive A. (The current file and description section of the Control Center should read *A:\MYFILES.CAT*.)
3. Open the AMOUNTS database so that its name is above the ruled line in the Control Center's Data panel.

Step 2   **Specify the Index.** When you have more than one index, as you do here, you can specify which index is to be used.

To specify an index

Press   SHIFT-F2 to display the database design screen, and the Organize menu is automatically pulled down

TABLE 24   New Record Added to Indexed File

Field	Data
ID:	**112**
DATE:	**06/19/90**
AMOUNT:	**20.00**

Press	O for *Order records by index* to display a list of available indexes
Highlight	*AMOUNT*, and then press ENTER
Press	F2 to display the file arranged by the index

Result.   The file is now arranged using the AMOUNT index.

Step 3   **Add a Record.** Now, add a new record to the indexed file.

To add a record on the Edit screen

Press	F2 (if necessary) to display the Edit screen
Press	ALT-R to pull down the Records menu
Press	A for *Add new records*

Result.   A blank record appears. Enter the record shown in Table 24. After entering the last field, press ↑. The new record immediately moves to the position specified by the index. It appears in the correct position for the file indexed by amount. (You may have to press PGUP one or more times to see it.)

Step 4   **Print Out the Records.** Make a printout of the records in the database file. Before proceeding, be sure that the printer is ready.

To print out the records

Press	ALT-E to pull down the Exit menu, and then press E for *Exit* to return to the Control Center
Press	SHIFT-F9 to display a submenu
Press	B for *Begin printing*

Result.   The records are printed out.

Step 5   **Continue or Quit.** You have now completed this tutorial. Either continue with the next tutorial or quit the program.

▼EXERCISES

EXERCISE 9A   Index the COURSES File

Index the COURSES file on the field you stored course titles in. Name the index TITLE, and specify an ascending order for the index. Display the file, and then print out a quick report.

EXERCISE 9B   Index the PLACEST File

Index the PLACEST file on the POP13086 field. Name the index CHANGE, and specify a descending order for the index. Display the file, and then print out a quick report. Table 12 describes the fields in the file.

QUESTIONS

1. What are two major advantages of using indexes? What is the primary disadvantage?
2. What is the difference between sorting and indexing a file?
3. Under what conditions can you use the Index key search command, and what does it do?

TOPIC 10
Querying the Database

▼CONCEPTS

In Topic 6, we introduced you to several commands that display records so that you can edit or delete them. Those commands were useful in a small database, but when the number of records increases, it becomes harder to find the record you want. For example, what if a customer calls about his or her account and wants to know what date a purchase was made? Using the customer ID number and the amount of the purchase, you can immediately locate the date of the purchase by asking the program to display any charges to the customer's account for the specified amount. Questions like this, when addressed to a database, are called queries. You can use queries to display, update, delete, and insert records into a database file. The records, or specified fields from the records, can be displayed on the screen or printed out in a report.

You query a database by entering criteria that filter the records. These are called view queries because you specify how the information in the database is to be viewed. You can use these view queries to examine selected records in the database, specify which records are printed on labels and reports, or to link files.

You specify criteria by specifying a value to look for in one or more fields. The value can be a text string, date, number, or logical value. The program searches the specified fields in all the records in the file. If it finds any matches, it displays the records that match the criteria. When the records are displayed, you can update or mark them for deletion. You can also specify that only selected fields from the records be displayed.

THE FILE AND VIEW SKELETONS

When you want to query a database, you first open the database file. You then highlight ⟨*create*⟩ on the Control Center's Queries panel, and press Enter to display the queries design screen (Figure 29). This screen has two parts: the file

FIGURE 29   The Queries Design Screen.   The queries design screen has two parts (a): the file skeleton and (b) the view skeleton.

A. The File Skeleton

B. The View Skeleton

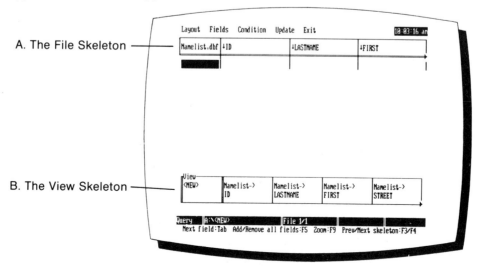

skeleton and the view skeleton. You can move the highlight between and around these two skeletons with the keys described later in Table 26.

The File Skeleton

The file skeleton displays the name of the file and the name of each field in that file. You use the file skeleton to enter criteria that specify which records are to be displayed. After entering your criteria, you press F2 to process it and display the records that match the criteria. The ↓ symbol preceding each field name indicates that a field will be displayed in the view when you process the query.

The View Skeleton

You use the view skeleton to specify which fields are to be displayed when you process a query. To add or delete fields from the view, you highlight the field's name on the file (or view) skeleton, and then press F5. The field disappears from the view skeleton, and the ↓ symbol on the file skeleton disappears or reappears. If you press F5 when the cursor is in the first column under the file's name, all fields are removed from the view or added back to it.

ENTERING FILTER CRITERIA

To enter criteria that filter records, you move the highlight to the field you want to filter, and then type in the criteria. To process the query, you then press F2 to display the Browse screen. You can then exit back to the Control Center, or press SHIFT-F2 to return to the queries design screen to enter additional queries. When entering queries, keep these basic rules in mind:

- Queries are case sensitive.
- Enter character strings (including numbers like ZIP codes, phone numbers, and ID numbers) in quotation marks. For example, to use the name Smith to filter records, enter it as **"Smith"**. To find the phone number 555-1007, enter it as **"555-1007"**.
- Enter numbers without quotation marks.
- Enter dates enclosed in braces ({}). For example, to enter January 1, 1992, enter it as **{01/01/92}**.
- Press CTRL-Y to delete previous queries in the field containing the highlight when the cursor is under the first character in the field.

USING AND AND OR CRITERIA

When you want to find records that match AND and OR criteria, you do so by positioning the criteria on rows.

- To specify an AND criteria, you enter all criteria in fields on the same row. Only those records that match both criteria are displayed. For example, to find all Smiths in California, enter **"Smith"** in the last name field, and enter **"CA"** in the state field on the same row.

    You can also specify an AND criteria in the same field by separating one or more criteria with commas. For example, to find all prices between 10 and 20, enter the query in the price field as >**10,** <**20**. To find all names from Smith to Thomas, enter the query as >=**"Smith"**, <=**"Thomas"**.
- To specify an OR criteria, you enter criteria on different rows. Records that match either criteria are displayed. For example, to find all Smiths in California or Texas, enter **"Smith"** in the last name field, and enter **"CA"** in the

state field on the same row. Then press ↓ and enter **"TX"** below the *"CA"* entry in the state field.

SORTING THE FILE

In Topic 8, you saw how you can sort a file to a new file. When querying the database, you can also sort them to the screen. To do so, you display the Queries screen, and then enter sorting operators into the fields you want to sort the file by. The sort operator does two things:

- The field that it is entered into determines the field used to rearrange the records. When the file is sorted based on a specific field, all the records are rearranged, not just the specified field.
- The type of operator determines the order of the sort. If you sort the numbers 0 to 9 in ascending order, they are arranged from 0 to 9; in descending order, they are arranged from 9 to 0. Table 20 shows the order in which letters are sorted when you select one of the sort orders listed on the menu.

If you want to sort on more than one field, you can do so by entering sort operators in more than one field. Enter codes in the sequence you want the fields sorted. The number following the code indicates the number of the key. The first code you enter is the field that is sorted first. When you enter sort operators, they are numbered in the sequence in which you enter them. These numbers indicate the order of the fields that will be used by the sort. The file will be sorted first by the field with the lowest number. It will then be sorted by the field with a code with the next lowest number, and so on. If you want, you can edit the numbers to change the order after entering the codes.

USING UPDATE OPERATORS

You use update operators to update all the records in a file that match a specified criteria. For example, you can add a number to all the numbers in a numeric field or change all the dates in a date field. When combined with criteria, this command can update groups of records that match the specified criteria. You can use any of the four update operators described in Table 25. To use them:

1. First enter a query that displays all the records that you want to update. Then press F2 to process the query to check the results.
2. Press SHIFT-F2 to return to the queries design screen, and then enter the operator under the filename in the first column on the file skeleton or select *Specify update operation* from the Update menu.
3. Enter the expression that performs the replace operation in the field you want replaced. It must be preceded by the word with. For example, to

TABLE 25   Update Operators

Operator	Description
Replace	Replaces all field entries in records that match the criteria entered into other fields on the file skeleton
Append	Appends records from one file to another when the files are linked
Mark	Marks all records for deletion that match the criteria entered into other fields on the file skeleton
Unmark	Unmarks all records for deletion that match the criteria entered into other fields on the file skeleton

95

increase amounts in the AMOUNT field by 10%, type **with AMOUNT*1.1**. To replace Smyth with Smith, type **with "Smith"**.

To enter the criteria and the update operator in the same field, separate them with a comma. For example, to update all prices that are $10 to $20, type **=10, with 20**.

4. Pull down the Update menu, and then select *Perform the update*. The file is not updated until you execute this command. If you leave the queries design screen before selecting it, the file remains unchanged.

If you save an update query, its name is listed on the Control Center's Queries panel preceded by an asterisk.

USING WILDCARDS AND OPERATORS IN QUERIES

You can use wildcards and operators to limit your search.

- To find characters embedded in a string, use the dollar sign operator (called the contains operator). For example, to find all records that contain the string "Street", type **$"Street"**.
- To use the * and ? wildcards, use the like operator. For example, to find all cities that begin with "New", type **like "New*"**.
- To find all entries that sound like the search string, use the sounds like operator. For example, to find all people whose name sounds like "Anne" or "Ann", type **Sounds like "Ann"**.

▼PROCEDURES

This section describes the procedures that you follow to:

- Enter a query
- Add and remove fields from view
- Use an existing query
- Use an update query
- Sort a database on the screen

To Enter a Query

1. Open the database file that you want to query.
2. Press TAB to move the highlight to the Queries panel, highlight ⟨*create*⟩, and then press ENTER to display the queries design screen (Figure 29).
3. Move the highlight to the field in which you want to enter the query using any of the commands described in Table 26.
4. Type the filter criteria.

TABLE 26   Queries Design Screen Cursor Movement and Editing Commands

To	Press
Move between file and view skeletons	F3 or F4
Move to the next field	TAB
Move to the previous field	BACKTAB
Move to the first field	HOME
Move to the last field	END
Delete the previous query	CTRL-Y
Process a query	F2
Return to the queries design screen from the Browse screen	SHIFT-F2

5. Press F2 to process the Query.
6. Press SHIFT-F2 to return to the queries design screen. (You can enter additional queries, or you can exit.)
7. Press ALT-E to pull down the Exit menu.
8. Either press S for *Saves changes and exit*, and the prompt reads *Save as:*. Type the name you want to save the query under, and then press ENTER to return to the Control Center.
   Or press A for *Abandon changes and exit*, and the prompt reads *Are you sure you want to abandon operation?*. Press Y to return to the Control Center.

To Add or Remove Fields from View

1. Open the database file that you want to query.
2. Press SHIFT-F2 to display the queries design screen.
3. Press TAB to move the highlight to the field's name on the file skeleton.
4. Either press F5.
   Or press ALT-F to pull down the Fields menu, and then press A for Add *field to view*, or press R for *Remove field from view*.

Use an Existing Query

1. Open the database file that you want to query.
2. Highlight the name of the query on the Control Center's Queries panel, and then press ENTER.
3. Highlight *Use view*, and then press ENTER.

To Update Records

1. Open the database file that you want to query.
2. Press TAB to move the highlight to the Queries panel, highlight ⟨*create*⟩, and then press ENTER. The cursor should be under the file's name on the file skeleton.
3. Use the commands described in Table 26 to move the highlight around the screen and enter the criteria you want to use to filter the records in the appropriate field(s).
4. Press F2 to process the query. Only the records to be affected should be displayed on the Browse screen.
5. Press SHIFT-F2 to return to the queries design screen.
6. Enter one of the update operators described in Table 24, and then press ENTER. The prompt reads *Changing this view query to an update query will delete the View skeleton*.
7. Press P for Proceed.
8. Type **with** followed by the dBASE expression in the field to be updated. For example, to increase prices in the PRICE field by 10%, enter with **PRICE*1.1** in the PRICE field.
9. Press Alt-U to pull down the Update menu, and then press P for Perform the update. The prompt reads Press any key to continue. Do so.
10. Press F2 twice to see the results.
11. Press ALT-E to pull down the Exit menu, and then press E for *Exit*. The prompt reads *Query design has been changed. Do you want to save it?*. Press Y and the prompt reads *Save as:*. Type the name of the file you want to save the query in, and then press ENTER to return to the Control Center. The query is listed on the Queries panel preceded with a asterisk.

TABLE 27   Sort Options

Option	Description	Code
Ascending ASCII	A..Z a..z 0..9	*Asc*
Descending ASCII	z..a Z..A 9..0	*Dsc*
Ascending Dictionary	Aa..Zz 0..9	*AscDict*
Descending Dictionary	zZ..aA 9..0	*DscDict*

To Sort a Database File on the Screen

1. Open the database that you want to sort.
2. Press TAB to move the highlight to the Queries panel, highlight ⟨*create*⟩, and then press ENTER.
3. Press TAB to move the highlight to the field that you want to sort on.
4. Press ALT-F to pull down the Fields menu.
5. Press S for *Sort on this field* to display a submenu.
6. Highlight one of the sort options described in Table 27, and then press ENTER. The field displays a code indicating the sort option that you selected. The number following the code indicates the number of the key.
7. To sort using a secondary key(s), repeat Steps 3 though 6.
8. Press F2 to process the query. The Browse screen is displayed with the records sorted in the specified order. (If the program had to create a separate file to display the data in sorted order, the status bar displays *ReadOnly* to indicate the file cannot be edited.)
9. Press ALT-E to pull down the Exit menu, and then press E for *Exit*. The prompt reads *Query design has been changed. Do you want to save it?*.
10. Press N to return to the Control Center.

▼TIPS

➤ **You can print a quick report after processing a query.** When the Browse screen is displayed, press SHIFT-F9 and then press B for *Begin printing*.

➤ **When entering long criteria in a field on the file skeleton**, you can press F9 to zoom the field open and then closed.

➤ **To see what fields have been indexed when the Queries screen is displayed**, set *Include indexes* on the Fields menu to *YES*. Fields for which indexes have been generated are preceded by a pound sign (#) on the file skeleton. If you have created any complex indexes (indexed on more than one field), they are added to the end of the file skeleton and are called pseudo-fields. You can enter criteria in these fields.

➤ **When you enter sort operators, they are numbered to indicate the sequence in which the file will be sorted.** If you change any of the operators in the same session, the numbering sequence continues. For example, if you sort the file by first name, the code may read *Asc1*. If you delete this code and enter a new one in another field, it will read *Asc2*. This does not mean that the field is sorted second. The sort always uses the field that currently has the lowest number as the basis for the sort.

TUTORIAL 10A
Querying the NAMELIST File

In this tutorial, you use criteria to filter records in the NAMELIST file.

Step 1   **Open the NAMELIST File.** Before proceeding:

1. Load dBASE so that the Control Center is displayed.
2. Insert your data disk into drive A, and then change the default drive to drive A. (The current file and description section of the Control Center should read *A:\MYFILES.CAT.*)
3. Open the NAMELIST database so that its name is above the ruled line in the Control Center's Data panel.

Step 2   **Display Records That Match a Single Criterion.** You can look for a group of records that matches a specific criterion. All fields in this file are character fields, so all criteria must be enclosed in double quotation marks. When using this command, the case you use for characters is also important; if a field has been entered as uppercase MA, lowercase ma will not display any records.

To display records that match a single criterion

Press	TAB to move the highlight to the Queries panel
Highlight	⟨*create*⟩, and then press ENTER
Press	TAB to move the highlight to the *ST* field on the file skeleton
Type	**"MA"** (Figure 30)
Press	F2 to process the query

Result.   The records that match the criterion are displayed. Print a quick report, and then press Shift-F2 to return to the queries design screen.

Step 3   **Remove Some Fields from View.** The last command displayed all the fields for the records that match the criteria. Here, you remove some fields from view.

To remove a field from view

Press	TAB to move the highlight to the *Namelist.dbf* column (the first column) on the file skeleton
Press	F5 to remove all fields from view. (All the ↓'s preceding their name are removed, and they no longer are displayed in the view skeleton.)

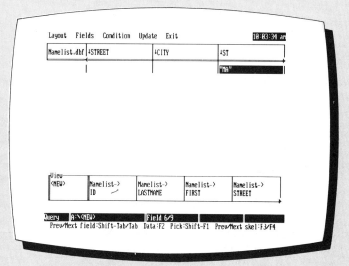

FIGURE 30   A Query on the Queries Design Screen.   Your query should look like this.

TOPIC

10

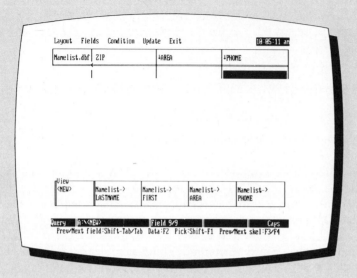

FIGURE 31 The View Skeleton with Fields Removed. Your view skeleton should look like this.

Press	TAB to move the highlight to the *LASTNAME* field, and then press F5 to add it to the view
Press	TAB to move the highlight to the *FIRST* field, and then press F5 to add it to the view
Press	TAB to move the highlight to the *AREA* field, and then press F5 to add it to the view
Press	TAB to move the highlight to the *PHONE* field, and then press F5 to add it to the view

Result. The view skeleton now lists only the four fields that are to be included in the view (Figure 31). Press F2 to process the query. The same records are displayed as in Step 2, but only the four specified fields are shown. Press SHIFT-F2 to return to the queries design screen. Press TAB to move the highlight to the *Namelist.dbf* column on the file skeleton, and then press F5 to add all fields back to the view.

Step 4 **Display Records Using an OR Query.** What if you want to find the records of the customers living in either Massachusetts or Texas? To do so, you use an OR criteria.

To use an OR query

Press	TAB to move the highlight to the *ST* field, and the criteria reads *"MA"*
Press	↓ to move the highlight down one row
Type	**"TX"**
Press	F2 to process the query

Result. The records that match the criteria of being from MA or TX are displayed. Print a quick report, and then press SHIFT-F2 to display the queries design screen.

Step 5 **Display Records Using an AND Query.** Now, display the records for all customers who live in Massachusetts and whose ID is greater than or equal to 105. (The 105 is enclosed in double quotation marks to indicate it is text.)

To use an AND query

Press	TAB to move the highlight to the *ST* field, and the criteria reads *"MA"* on one row and *"TX"* on the next
Highlight	the criteria *"TX"*
Press	CTRL-Y to delete the filter

Press	↑ to move the cursor up one row to highlight "MA"
Press	TAB to move the highlight to the *ID* field
Type	>="105"
Press	F2 to process the query

Result. Two records match the criteria of living in MA and having an ID equal to or greater than 105.

Step 6 **Save the Query.** Whenever you have a query that you want to reuse, you can save it. Here, let's save the query you just entered.

To save a query

Press	SHIFT-F2 to return to the queries design screen
Press	ALT-L to pull down the layout menu
Press	S for *Save this query*, and the prompt reads *Save as:*
Type	**QUERY**1 and then press ENTER

Result. The query's name is listed on the view skeleton. It will be listed in the Queries panel when you return to the Control Center.

Step 7 **Continue to Experiment.** You might want to experiment with some other queries before proceeding. Remember to delete existing queries with the CTRL-Y command before entering new ones. When you are finished, press ALT-E to pull down the Exit menu, and then press A for *Abandon changes* and exit.

Step 8 **Continue or Quit.** You have now completed this tutorial. Either continue with the next tutorial or quit the program. (If you toggled the printer on to make a printout of the results of your commands, press CTRL-P now to toggle the printer off.)

TUTORIAL 10B
Querying the AMOUNTS File

In this tutorial, you use relational and logical operators to find records in the AMOUNTS file.

Step 1 **Open the AMOUNTS File.** Before proceeding:

1. Load dBASE so that the Control Center is displayed.
2. Insert your data disk into drive A, and then change the default drive to drive A. (The current file and description section of the Control Center should read *A:\MYFILES.CAT*.)
3. Open the AMOUNTS database so that its name is above the ruled line in the Control Center's Data panel.

Step 2 **Display Records That Match a Single Criterion.** You can look for a group of records that matches a specific criterion.

To display records that match a single criterion

Press	TAB to move the highlight to the Queries panel
Highlight	⟨create⟩, and then press ENTER
Press	TAB to move the highlight to the *AMOUNT* field on the file skeleton

Type   **50**
Press   F2 to process the query

Result.   The record matching the criterion is displayed. Print a quick report, and then press SHIFT-F2 to display the queries design screen.

Step 3   **Display Selected Fields from Records That Match One Criterion.** Now repeat the previous command, but this time specify that only the DATE and AMOUNT fields are to be displayed, and the criterion is all amounts equal to 15.

To remove a field from view
Press   TAB to move the highlight to the *ID* field on the file skeleton, and then press F5 to remove it from view

To specify the criteria
Press   TAB to move the highlight to the *AMOUNT* field
Type   **15**
Press   F2 to process the query

Result.   The DATE and AMOUNT fields for the record that matches the criterion of an amount of 15 is displayed. Print a quick report, and then press SHIFT-F2 to return to the queries design screen. Press TAB to move the highlight to the *Amounts.dbf* column, and then press F5 to add all fields back to the view.

Step 4   **Display Records Using an AND Query.** Now, find all records that have dates after June 11, 1990, and amounts greater than 20. Dates must be enclosed in braces ({}) to work.

To display records using an AND query
Press   TAB to move the highlight to the *DATE* field
Type   **{06/14/90}**
Press   F2 to process the query

Result.   The one record with a date of June 14, 1990, and an amount of 15 is displayed. Press ALT-E to pull down the Exit menu, and then press E for *Exit*. The prompt reads *Query design has been changed. Do you want to save it?*. Press N to return to the Control Center.

Step 5   **Continue or Quit.** You have now completed this tutorial. Either continue with the next tutorial or quit the program.

TUTORIAL 10C
Sorting the NAMELIST File

In this tutorial, you sort the NAMELIST file on the screen.

Step 1   **Open the NAMELIST File.** Before proceeding:

1. Load dBASE so that the Control Center is displayed.
2. Insert your data disk into drive A, and then change the default drive to drive A. (The current file and description section of the Control Center should read *A:\MYFILES.CAT*.)
3. Open the NAMELIST database so that its name is above the ruled line in the Control Center's Data panel.

Step 2   **Sort the File in Ascending Order.** A file can easily be sorted on any field. Let's sort the file alphabetically by the LASTNAME field.

To sort the file in ascending order

Press	TAB to move the highlight to the Queries panel, highlight ⟨*create*⟩, and then press ENTER
Highlight	the *LASTNAME* field on the file skeleton
Press	ALT-F to pull down the Fields menu, and then press S for *Sort on this field*
Highlight	*Ascending ASCII*, and then press ENTER. The code *Asc1* is displayed in the *LASTNAME* field
Press	F2 to process the query

Result.   The drive spins as the file is sorted. In a moment the Browse screen is displayed with the records sorted alphabetically by last name in ascending order.

Step 3   **Sort the File in Descending Order.** Now, sort the file in descending order.

To sort the file in descending order

Press	SHIFT-F2 to display the queries design screen
Highlight	the *LASTNAME* field on the file skeleton
Press	CTRL-Y to delete the current entry
Press	ALT-F to pull down the Fields menu, and then press S for *Sort on this field*
Highlight	*Descending ASCII*, and then press ENTER. The code *Dsc2* is displayed in the *LASTNAME* field
Press	F2 to process the query

Result.   The drive spins as the file is sorted. In a moment, the Browse screen is displayed with the records sorted alphabetically by last name in descending order. The status bar displays *ReadOnly* to indicate that you cannot edit this file.

Step 4   **Sort the File on More Than One Field.** You can specify that the file be sorted by more than one field. Here, sort the file first by ZIP code and then by last name.

To sort the file by more than one field

Press	SHIFT-F2 to display the queries design screen
Press	TAB to move the highlight to the *LASTNAME* field on the file skeleton
Press	CTRL-Y to delete the current entry
Press	TAB to move the highlight to the *ZIP* field on the file skeleton
Press	ALT-F to pull down the Fields menu, and then press S for *Sort on this field*
Highlight	*Ascending ASCII*, and then press ENTER. The code *Asc3* is displayed in the *ZIP* field
Press	TAB to move the highlight to the *LASTNAME* field
Press	ALT-F to pull down the Fields menu, and then press S for *Sort on this field*
Highlight	*Ascending ASCII*, and then press ENTER. The code *Asc4* is displayed in the *LASTNAME* field
Press	F2 to process the query

Result.   The drive spins as the file is sorted. In a moment, the Browse screen is displayed with the records sorted first by ZIP code and then by last name. If you look at the records with ZIP codes of 20000, you will see that the last names for those ZIP codes are in ascending order. Print out a quick report.

103

Step 5 Continue or Quit. You have now completed this tutorial. Either continue with the next tutorial or quit the program. Press ALT-E to pull down the Exit menu, and then press E for *Exit*. The prompt reads *Query design has been changed. Do you want to save it?*. Press N to return to the Control Center.

TUTORIAL 10D
Replacing Values in the AMOUNTS File

In this tutorial, you replace values in the AMOUNTS file.

Step 1 Open the AMOUNTS File. Before proceeding:

1. Load dBASE so that the Control Center is displayed.
2. Insert your data disk into drive A, and then change the default drive to drive A. (The current file and description section of the Control Center should read *A:\MYFILES.CAT.*)
3. Open the AMOUNTS database so that its name is above the ruled line in the Control Center's Data panel.

Step 2 Replace Values. Let's increase all values in the AMOUNTS field by 10% if the date of the charge was prior to 6/11/90.

To replace values

Press	TAB to move the highlight to the Queries panel, highlight <*create*>, and then press ENTER. The cursor should be under the file's name
Type	**Replace** and then press ENTER. The prompt reads *Changing this view query to an update query will delete the View skeleton*
Press	P for *Proceed*
Press	TAB to move the highlight to the *DATES* field on the file skeleton
Type	<{06/11/90}
Press	TAB to move the highlight to the *AMOUNT* field on the file skeleton
Type	**with AMOUNT∗1.1**
Press	ALT-U to pull down the Update menu, and then press P for *Perform the update*
Press	F2 twice to see the results

Result.   The records dated earlier than 6/11/90 have been increased by 10%. (You may have to press PGUP to see them.) Print a quick report.

Step 3 Exit and Save the Query. Whenever you have a query that you want to reuse, you can save it. Here, let's save the query you just entered as you exit the update query design screen.

To save a query

Press	ALT-E to pull down the Exit menu
Press	E for *Exit* and the prompt reads *Query design has been changed. Do you want to save it?*
Press	Y and the prompt reads *Save as:*
Type	**UPDATE** and then press ENTER to return to the Control Center

Result. The query is listed on the Queries panel as *UPDATE*. The asterisk preceding the name indicates that it is an update query.

Step 4 Continue or Quit. You have now completed this tutorial. Either continue with the next tutorial or quit the program.

▼EXERCISES

EXERCISE 10A   Query the COURSES File

Open the COURSES file, and then enter the following queries. When you process the query and the Browse screen is displayed, print a quick report of the results.

1. Display all courses that are held on Mondays. (You query logical fields by entering .**T.** or .**F.**)
2. Display the course(s) that are held at 8:00 am.

EXERCISE 10B   Query the PLACEST File

Open the PLACEST file, and then enter the following queries. When you process the query and the Browse screen is displayed, print a quick report of the results. Table 12 describes the fields in the file.

1. Display the record for Iowa.
2. Display the states with an entry in the POP01080 field of 7365011.

▼QUESTIONS

1. What are criteria? What do they do?
2. What is the file skeleton? What purpose does it serve?
3. What is the view skeleton? What purpose does it serve?
4. Do all queries display complete records that match the criteria?
5. How do you enter criteria? List some of the rules that criteria must follow.
6. How do you enter an OR query? An AND query?
7. How do you sort the file on the screen?
8. What is an update operator? What steps do you follow to enter one?

▼ CONCEPTS

You can expand the power of queries by using relational operators to select records and summary operators to make calculations.

RELATIONAL OPERATORS

Relational operators are used to test two or more numbers to determine their relationship. Table 28 describes dBASE's relational operators. Using these operators, you can determine if one number is equal to, less than, or greater than another number. Let's say, for example, that you are comparing last year's sales to this year's:

- Equal to. If you use a relational operator to determine if last year's sales are equal to this year's, the sales for both years must be the same for the statement to be true. In all other situations, the statement is false.

TABLE 28   Relational Operators

Operator	Description
>	Finds all records greater than the criteria you specify. For example, **NAME>JONES** displays all records alphabetically after JONES; **AMOUNT>10.00** finds all records where the AMOUNT is more than 10.00; and **DATE>1/10/89** finds all records where the DATE is later than January 10, 1989.
<	Finds all records less than the criteria you specify. For example, **NAME<JONES** displays all records alphabetically before JONES; **AMOUNT<10.00** finds all records where the AMOUNT is less than 10.00; and **DATE<1/10/85** finds all records where the DATE is earlier than January 10, 1985.
=	Finds all records equal to the criteria you specify. For example, **LASTNAME=JONES** finds all records with JONES in the LASTNAME field; **AMOUNT=10.00** finds all records where the AMOUNT is 10.00; and **DATE=1/10/89** finds all records dated January 10, 1989.
>=	Finds all records greater than or equal to the criteria you specify. For example, **LASTNAME>=JONES** finds all records with JONES or any name alphabetically later in the LASTNAME field; **AMOUNT>=10.00** finds all records where the AMOUNT is 10.00 or more; and **DATE>=1/10/89** finds all records where the DATE is January 10, 1989, or later.
<=	Finds all records less than or equal to the criteria you specify. For example, **LASTNAME<=JONES** finds all records with JONES or any name alphabetically earlier in the LASTNAME field; **AMOUNT<=10.00** finds all records where the AMOUNT is 10.00 or less; and **DATE<=1/10/89** finds all records where the DATE is January 10, 1989, or earlier.
<> or #	Finds all records not equal to the criteria you specify. For example, **LASTNAME<>JONES** finds all records except those with JONES in the LASTNAME field; **AMOUNT<>10.00** finds all records where the AMOUNT is not 10.00; and **DATE<>1/10/90** finds all records not dated January 10, 1990.

- Greater than. If you use a relational operator to determine if last year's sales are greater than this year's, the sales for last year must be greater than this year's for the statement to be true. In all other situations, the statement is false.
- Less than. If you use a relational operator to determine if last year's sales were less than this year's, the sales for last year must be less than this year's for the statement to be true. In all other situations, the statement is false.
- Equal to or greater than. If you use a relational operator to determine if last year's sales were equal to or greater than this year's, the sales for last year must be equal to or less than this year's for the statement to be true. In all other situations, the statement is false.
- Equal to or less than. If you use a relational operator to determine if last year's sales were equal to or less than this year's, the sales for last year must be equal to or less than this year's for the statement to be true. In all other situations, the statement is false.

If you want to use AND queries, you can enter them in the same field separated by commas. For example, entering **>50, <100** will filter records so that those with amounts greater than 50 and less than 100 are displayed.

SUMMARY OPERATORS

You can enter queries that calculate selected fields in one or more records. To do so, you enter functions into the queries. For example, to sum the numbers in the AMOUNT field, you enter the summary operator **SUM** in the AMOUNT field. You can also sum selected records by filtering them with criteria entered in other fields. When you press F2 to process the query, only the calculated result is displayed; all the other fields are empty. Table 29 describes the summary operators that you can use.

TIP

► **You can print a quick report when the queries design screen is displayed.** To do so, press SHIFT-F9 and then press B for *Begin printing*.

TABLE 29   Summary Operators

Function	Description
AVERAGE	Calculates the average in a specified numeric or float field
SUM	Calculates the total in a specified numeric field
COUNT	Counts the number of records that meet a specified criterion
MIN	Indicates the lowest value in a numeric, float, character, or date field
MAX	Indicates the highest value in a numeric, float, character, or date field

TUTORIAL 11A
Querying the NAMELIST File with Relational Operators

In this tutorial, you use relational operators to find records in the NAMELIST file.

Step 1 **Open the NAMELIST File.** Before proceeding:
1. Load dBASE so that the Control Center is displayed.
2. Insert your data disk into drive A, and then change the default drive to drive A. (The current file and description section of the Control Center should read *A:\MYFILES.CAT.*)
3. Open the NAMELIST database so that its name is above the ruled line in the Control Center's Data panel.

Step 2 **Display Records That Match a Single Criterion.** You can use relational operators to filter out records that match a specific criterion, for example, states greater than MA.

To display records that match a single criterion

Press	TAB to move the highlight to the Queries panel
Highlight	<*create*>, and then press ENTER
Press	TAB to move the highlight to the *ST* field
Type	>"MA"
Press	F2 to display the browse screen

Result. The records that are less than MA are displayed. Press SHIFT-F2 to display the queries design screen. Revise the query so that it reads >="MA", and then process the query. This time files with MA in the state field are included. Print out a quick report, and then return to the queries design screen.

Step 3 **Display Records Using an OR Query.** What if you want to find the records of the customers living in just the states NJ OR MA?

To use an OR query

Highlight	the *ST* field, and the criteria reads >="MA"
Press	CTRL-Y to delete the criteria
Type	"NJ"
Press	↓ to move the highlight down one row
Type	"MA"
Press	F2 to process the query

Result. The records that match the criteria are displayed. Press SHIFT-F2 to display the queries design screen.

Step 4 **Display Records Using an AND Query.** Now, display the records for all customers who live in states greater than CT AND less than MA.

To use an AND query

Highlight	the *ST* field, and the criteria reads "NJ" on the first row and "MA" on the row below
Highlight	"MA", and then press CTRL-Y to delete the filter
Highlight	"NJ", and then type >"CT", <"MA" over it
Press	F2 to process the query

Result. The records greater than CT and less than MA are displayed. Press SHIFT-F2 to display the queries design screen.

Step 5 **Display Records Using a NOT Query.** Now, display the records for all customers who live in states greater than CT AND less than MA.

To use an AND query

Highlight	the *ST* field, and the criteria reads >*"CT"*, <*"MA"*
Press	CTRL-Y to delete the filter
Type	**<>"MA"**
Press	F2 to process the query

Result. The records not from MA are displayed.

Step 6 **Continue to Experiment.** Table 28 lists relational operators. You might want to experiment with some of these before proceeding. If you make any mistakes, the program will respond with an error message and may ask if you want help. When you are finished, use the Exit menu to abandon your queries, and then return to the Control Center.

Step 7 **Continue or Quit.** You have now completed this tutorial. Either continue with the next tutorial or quit the program.

TUTORIAL 11B
Querying the AMOUNTS File with Relational and Summary Operators

In this tutorial, you use relational and summary operators to find records in the AMOUNTS file.

Step 1 **Open the AMOUNTS File.** Before proceeding:

1. Load dBASE so that the Control Center is displayed.
2. Insert your data disk into drive A, and then change the default drive to drive A. (The current file and description section of the Control Center should read *A:\MYFILES.CAT*.)
3. Open the AMOUNTS database so that its name is above the ruled line in the Control Center's Data panel.

Step 2 **Display Records That Match a Single Criterion.** Let's look for records with amounts greater than or equal to 50.

To display records that match a single criterion

Press	TAB to move the highlight to the Queries panel
Highlight	*<create>*, and then press ENTER
Press	TAB to move the highlight to the *AMOUNT* field
Type	**>=50**
Press	F2 to process the query

Result. The records with amounts greater than or equal to 50 are displayed. Press SHIFT-F2 to display the queries design screen.

Step 3 **Display Records Using an AND Criteria.** Now, find all records that have dates between June 11, 1990, and June 14, 1990. Dates must be enclosed in braces ({}) to work.

To display records using an AND criteria

Highlight	the *AMOUNT* field, and then press CTRL-Y to delete the entry
Press	TAB to move the highlight to the *DATE* field

Press	F9 to zoom the field open
Type	>={06/11/90}, <={06/14/90}
Press	F9 to zoom the field closed
Press	F2 to process the query

Result. The records between the two dates are displayed. Press SHIFT-F2 to return to the queries design screen. Move the highlight to the DATE field, and then press CTRL-Y to delete the criteria.

Step 4 **Total the Amounts Due.** To make calculations, you enter a summary operator into the field that you want calculated.

To total amounts

Highlight	the *AMOUNT* field
Type	**SUM**
Press	F2 to process the query

Result. The Browse screen is displayed with the total of all amounts in the AMOUNT field.

Step 5 **Average the Amounts Due.** Now, average the same field.

To average amounts

Press	SHIFT-F2 to display the queries design screen
Highlight	the *AMOUNT* field, and then press CTRL-Y to delete the current entry
Type	**AVG**
Press	F2 to process the query

Result. The Browse screen is displayed with the average of all amounts in the AMOUNT field.

Step 6 **Find the Maximum Amount Due.** Now, find the maximum amount due.

To find the maximum amount

Press	SHIFT-F2 to display the queries design screen
Highlight	the *AMOUNT* field, and then press CTRL-Y to delete the current entry
Type	**MAX**
Press	F2 to process the query

Result. The Browse screen is displayed with the maximum amount due. Press ALT-E to pull down the Exit menu, and then press A for *Abandon changes and exit.* The prompt reads *Are you sure you want to abandon operation?.* Press Y to return to the Control Center.

Step 7 **Continue or Quit.** You have now completed this tutorial. Either continue with the next tutorial or quit the program.

▼ EXERCISE

EXERCISE 11A   Query the PLACEST File

Open the PLACEST file, and then enter the following queries. When you process the query and the Browse screen is displayed, print a quick report of each query. Table 12 describes the fields in the file.

1. Display all states with populations in the POP01080 field greater than 10 million.
2. Display all states with a population change in the POP13086 field that is less than or equal to zero.
3. Display all states with a population change in the POP13086 field that is less than zero or greater than 19.
4. Display the states with an entry in the POP01080 field greater than 10,000,000. How many are there?
5. Display the states with an entry in the POP01080 field greater than 10,000,000 AND an entry in the POP13086 field greater than 5 (5%). How many are there?
6. Display the states with entries in the POP01080 field between 5,000,000 and 8,000,000. How many are there?
7. Display the states with entries in the POP01080 field less than 1,000,000 OR greater than 20,000,000. How many are there?
8. Repeat questions 4 through 7 but use the POP01086 field instead of the POP01080 field.
9. SUM the total population in the following fields:
   - POP01080
   - POP01086

▼ QUESTIONS

1. What are relational operators? List and describe some.
2. Assume you have a list of charges with DATE and AMOUNT fields. Indicate the field(s) and the criteria you would enter for each of the following queries:
   - Dates on or before January 1, 1990
   - Dates after January 1, 1990
   - Amounts equal to or less than $50.00
   - Amounts greater than $50.00 charged before January 1, 1900
3. List and describe some of the summary operators you can use to make calculations.

▼ **CONCEPTS**

Once you have a database file, you use it to print mailing labels, envelopes, ID badges, or almost any other type of label. To do so, you open the database file you want to use. You then highlight <*create*> in the Control Center's Labels panel, and then press ENTER. This displays the labels design screen (Figure 32).

The box in the center of the screen represents the label that you are going to create. The shaded area is called a layout work surface. (We discuss this surface in more detail in Topic 13.) To design a label, you follow these steps:

1. Select a label dimension.
2. Move the cursor to the position where you want to add a field, and then use the *Add fields* choice on the Fields menu to add the field. Its position is indicated by a field template (*XXXXX*).
   - You can select the field templates and then copy or move them to other positions on the layout surface. You can also add text as described in Topic 13.
   - The layout surface is initially filled with blanks that appear shaded. When you enter field templates, they replace these blanks in their position. If you enter text or press SPACEBAR, you enter characters. These characters appear against a black background (or a different color on a color display) so that you can distinguish them from blanks. To replace characters with blanks, just delete the characters with DEL or BACKSPACE.
3. Format the label. To do so, you first select it as described in the box "Selecting Items." After selecting a block, you can also pull down the Words menu to assign formats (see Table 34 in Topic 13) or the Display menu to assign colors.
4. Save the label format. If you want to use the label format again, you can save it so that it is listed on the Control Center's Labels panel.
5. Print the labels. But first, to be sure they will print correctly, either print a sample label to check your results or view the labels on the screen.

FIGURE 32   The Labels Design Screen.   The labels design screen contains a box with a layout work surface. You move the cursor around this box and use the Add fields choice on the Fields menu to specify what fields are to print on the label and where they are to print.

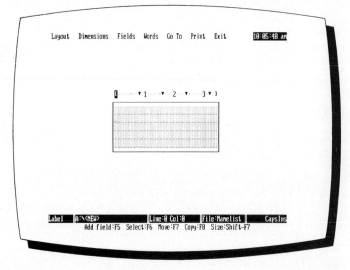

Selecting Items

When working on a layout work surface, you can select items. After selecting an item, you can delete, copy, move, size, or format it.

- To select items, move the cursor to the beginning of the block, press F6 and then use the arrow keys to expand the highlight. Press ENTER to confirm the selection. You can also press F6 twice to select a word or field, or three times to select a paragraph.
- To remove the highlight without making a selection, press ESC.
- To delete the selection, press DEL.
- To move the selection, move the cursor to where you want it moved, and then press F7.
- To copy the selection, move the cursor

to where you want it copied, and then press F8.
- To size a field or box, press SHIFT-F7 and then use the arrow keys to change its size. Press ENTER to complete the procedure.
- To format the selection, pull down the Words menu, and then make one or more choices (see Table 34 in Topic 13).

If you select an item on the layout surface, and then copy or move it, a ghost image indicating the size of the selection appears in the new position so that you can make final adjustments. You then press ENTER to complete the copy or move process. Anything in the new position is overwritten. If you moved the block, the original position is blanked and appears shaded.

▼PROCEDURES

This section describes the procedures that you follow to:

- Lay out and print labels

To Display the Labels Design Screen

1. Open the database file you want to create labels for.
2. Press TAB to move the highlight to the Labels panel.
3. Highlight <create>, and then press ENTER to display the labels design screen (Figure 32).

To Specify a Label's Dimensions

1. Display the labels design screen.
2. Press ALT-D to pull down the Dimensions menu.
3. Make any of the menu choices described in Table 30.

To Add Fields to the Label

1. Display the labels design screen.
2. Use the arrow keys to move the cursor to where you want the field positioned on the label.
3. Either press ALT-F to pull down the Fields menu, and then press A for *Add field* to display a list of field names you can choose from. (You can also make any of the other selections described in Table 31.)
   Or press F5 to display the list of field names.

113

TABLE 30   The Dimensions Menu

Menu Choice	Description
Predefined sizes	Displays a submenu listing many common predesigned sizes. The first two numbers indicate the label's size. The third number indicates the number of labels across the page. To select one, highlight it, and then press ENTER.
Width of label	Allows you to specify your own label width.
Height of label	Allows you to specify the maximum number of lines on a label.
Indentation	Allows you to specify the left margin.
Lines between labels	Allows you to specify the number of lines between your labels.
Space between label columns	Allows you to specify the distance between your labels.
Columns of labels	Allows you to specify the number of labels across the page.

TABLE 31   The Fields Menu

Menu Choice	Description
Add field	Displays a submenu of the fields that you can choose from. Highlight the one you want to use, and then press ENTER to display a box that allows you to specify an optional template or picture function. • *Template* displays a submenu that allows you to modify a template so that only the specified type of data can be entered into the field. You can also add commas in a numeric field to print thousands separators on reports. For example, a template 99999 prints 12345, but a template 99,999 prints 12,345. • *Picture functions* displays a submenu that allows you to specify picture functions for a field. When you press CTRL-END to save the settings, a field template is inserted into the band at the cursor's position. When you print the report, data from each record in the database is printed in the position of the template.
Remove field	Removes the current field or allows you to select from a list of fields to be removed.
Modify field	Allows you to modify the way your fields print using the template or picture functions. • *Template* (see "Add field" above) • *Picture function* (see "Add field" above)
Change hidden field	Allows you to modify hidden calculated or summary fields if the label has them.

4. Highlight the desired field name, and then press ENTER to display a dialog box. (If you want to specify a template or picture function, see Table 31.)
5. Press CTRL-END to save the settings and insert a template onto the label work surface.
6. Repeat Steps 2 through 4 for each field that you want printed on the label.

To Format Fields

1. Display the labels design screen for the labels.
2. Use the arrow keys to move the cursor to where you want the field positioned on the label.
3. Move the cursor to the beginning of the field that you want to format.
4. Press F6, use the arrow keys to expand the highlight over all the text you want formatted, and then press ENTER.
5. Press ALT-W to pull down the Words menu, and then press S for *Style* to display a submenu.
6. Highlight any of the formats listed on the menu, and then press ENTER.

To Save the Label Format

1. Press ALT-L to pull down the Layout menu. (You can select the *Edit description* of label design to add a description before saving.)
2. Press S for *Save this label design*, and the prompt reads *Save as:*.
3. Type the name of the label, and then press ENTER.

To Print the Labels

1. Display the labels design screen for the labels.
2. Press ALT-P to pull down the Print menu.
3. Make any of the selections described in Table 32.
4. Either press B for *Begin printing* to print the labels.

   Or   press G for *Generate sample labels* to test your settings.

   Or   press V for *View labels on screen* to see how the labels look.

TABLE 32   The Print Menu

Menu Choice	Description
Begin printing	Sends the report to the printer. (You can press CTRL-S to temporarily pause printing or ESC to cancel it. If you pause, press any key to resume.)
Eject page now	Ejects the page from the printer.
Generate sample labels	Prints a sample label so that you can check the results before printing all the labels.
View report on screen	Displays the report on the screen so that you can preview the results before sending it to the printer.
Use print form	Selects a profile of printer settings that you previously created and saved.
Save settings to print form	Lets you save your settings or modify them for future use.
Destination	Specifies where the report is to be sent. You can send it to the printer or to a DOS text file. Switch between the options with SPACEBAR.
Control of printer	Sends instructions to the printer regarding print quality and paging.
Output options	Specifies the pages to be printed, page numbers, and the number of copies.
Page dimensions	Specifies the length of the page (in lines), the offset from the left margin, and line spacing.

▼**TIPS**

➤ **After saving a label format, you can modify the design** using the same procedures you used to create it. To display the labels design screen, highlight the file's name on the Control Center. Then press SHIFT-F2 or press ENTER and then select *Modify layout* from the submenu that appears.

➤ **Two of the menus on the labels design screen are described in other topics.** The Words menu is described in Table 34 (see Topic 13), and the Go To menu is described in Table 15 (see Topic 6).

➤ **To remove blank spaces from labels and reports so that large gaps are not left when the labels or reports are printed,** you do two things:

1. Turn on the Trim function. To do so, pull down the Fields menu on the labels design screen, and then select *Modify field.* If *Trim* is *OFF*, press T to turn it on, and then press CTRL-END to return to the labels design screen.
2. Move the cursor to all the shaded blank areas between the field templates, and then press SPACEBAR to replace the blanks with spaces. When you now print the labels, the spaces will be trimmed so that the words print together.

TUTORIAL 12A
Printing Labels from the NAMELIST File

In this tutorial, you print a report for the NAMELIST file.

Step 1   **Open the NAMELIST File.** Before proceeding:

1. Load dBASE so that the Control Center is displayed.
2. Insert your data disk into drive A, and then change the default drive to drive A. (The current file and description section of the Control Center should read *A:\MYFILES.CAT*.)
3. Open the NAMELIST database so that its name is above the ruled line in the Control Center's Data panel.

Step 2   **Display the Labels Design Screen.** Once you have created a database file, you can display the labels design screen to create your labels.

To display the labels design screen
Press   TAB to move the highlight to the Labels panel, highlight *<create>*, and then press ENTER

Result.   The labels design screen is displayed (Figure 32).

Step 3   **Specify the Label's Dimensions.** Let's begin by selecting a standard label design from the list of predefined labels. We'll choose one that prints labels one after the other on the page.

To specify the label's dimensions
Press   ALT-D to pull down the dimensions menu
Press   P for *Predefined Size* to display a submenu listing available sizes
Press   1 for *15/16 × 3 1/2 X 1*

Result.   The cursor returns to the label box.

Step 4   **Add Fields.** Now, you specify what fields are to be printed and where they are to be positioned on the label. As you follow these steps, watch the status bar since it indicates the position of the cursor by line and column. You use the arrow keys to move the cursor so that the status bar indicates the correct position, and then follow the instructions.

Note.   Be sure to use the arrow keys (or HOME and END) to move the cursor around the label box. Pressing SPACEBAR changes blanks to spaces, and pressing ENTER moves fields down a line.

To add the first name field
Move   the cursor so that the status bar reads *Line: 0 Col:0*
Press   ALT-F to pull down the Fields menu, and then press A for *Add field*
Highlight   *FIRST*, and then press ENTER to display a submenu
Press   CTRL-END to save the setting and return to the label box

To add the last name field
Move   the cursor so that the status bar reads *Line: 0 Col:9*
Press   ALT-F to pull down the Fields menu, and then press A for *Add field*
Highlight   *LASTNAME*, and then press ENTER to display a submenu
Press   CTRL-END to save the setting and return to the label box

117

To add the street field

Move	the cursor so that the status bar reads *Line: 1 Col:0*
Press	ALT-F to pull down the Fields menu, and then press A for *Add field*
Highlight	*STREET*, and then press ENTER to display a submenu
Press	CTRL-END to save the setting and return to the label box

To add the city field

Move	the cursor so that the status bar reads *Line: 2 Col:0*
Press	ALT-F to pull down the Fields menu, and then press A for *Add field*
Highlight	*CITY*, and then press ENTER to display a submenu
Press	CTRL-END to save the setting and return to the label box
Type	, (a comma)

To add the state field

Move	the cursor so that the status bar reads *Line: 2 Col:12*
Press	ALT-F to pull down the Fields menu, and then press A for *Add field*
Highlight	*ST*, and then press ENTER to display a submenu
Press	CTRL-END to save the setting and return to the label box

To add the ZIP code field

Move	the cursor so that the status bar reads *Line: 2 Col:15*
Press	ALT-F to pull down the Fields menu, and then press A for *Add field*
Highlight	*ZIP*, and then press ENTER to display a submenu
Press	CTRL-END to save the setting and return to the label box

Result. Your screen should look like the one in Figure 33.

Step 5 **Format Fields.** To format fields, you select them and then use the Words menu to assign formats. Let's boldface the person's name.

To format fields

Move	the cursor to under the first character in the first field template. The status bar reads *Line: 0 Col: 0*
Press	F6 to turn extend selection on
Press	END to move the cursor to the end of the line
Press	ENTER to complete the selection

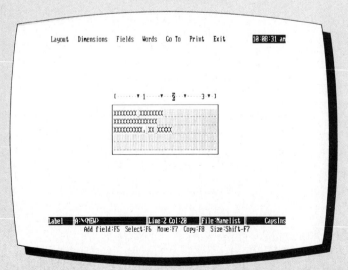

FIGURE 33 The Finished Label. When you are finished, your label design should look like this.

Press	Alt-W to pull down the Words menu, and then press S for *Style* to display a submenu
Press	B for *Bold*

Result. No change is seen on the screen.

Step 6 **Save the Format.** Now that the format is finished, save it so that you can use it again.

To save the format

Press	Alt-L to pull down the Layout menu
Press	S for *Save this label design,* and the prompt reads *Save as:*
Type	**LABEL1** and then press Enter

Result. The drive spins as the label format is saved.

Step 7 **View the Labels on the Screen.** Let's preview the labels on the screen.

To view the labels on the screen

Press	Alt-P to pull down the Print menu
Press	V for *View labels on screen*

Result. The drive spins, and in a few moments, the labels are displayed on the screen. Press Spacebar to view more labels, and then press Esc to return to the labels design screen.

Step 8 **Print the Labels.** Now, send the labels to the printer. Before proceeding, be sure the printer is ready.

To print the labels

Press	Alt-P to pull down the Print menu
Press	B for *Begin printing*

Result. The labels are printed out, and the names on the first line are boldfaced. Notice how there are large gaps between some of the words. This is because each field reserves a fixed space.

Step 9 **Use the Trim Function to Remove Spaces.** If you turn the Trim function on, and replace the shaded blanks on the layout surface with spaces, any extra spaces will be trimmed when you print the labels.

To turn Trim on

Highlight	the *FIRST* template in the upper left-hand corner of the box
Press	Alt-F to pull down the Fields menu, and then press M for *Modify*
Press	P for *Picture functions* to display a submenu. If *Trim* is *ON,* press Esc. If *Trim* is *OFF,* press T to turn it on. Then press Ctrl-End to save the setting
Press	Ctrl-End to save the changes

Result. The cursor returns to the labels design surface. Now, move the cursor to the shaded blanks between the fields, and then press Spacebar to replace the shaded blanks with spaces. When you do so, the shaded area turns black when highlighted by the cursor. Your finished design should look like Figure 34.

Step 10 **Print the Labels.** Now, print the labels again.

To print the labels

Press	Alt-P to pull down the Print menu
Press	B for *Begin printing*

119

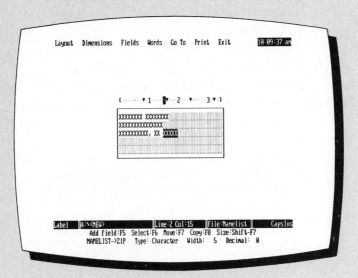

FIGURE 34 Label with Blanks Removed. When you are finished, your label design should look like this.

Result. The labels are printed out. There are no longer large gaps between some of the words.

Step 11 **Return to the Control Center.** Now, return to the Control Center.

To return to the Control Center

Press ALT-E to pull down the Exit menu, and then press S for *Saves changes and exit*

Result. The label format that you saved is listed in the Control Center's Labels panel.

Step 12 **Continue or Quit.** You have now completed this tutorial. Either continue with the next tutorial or quit the program.

▼ EXERCISE

EXERCISE 12A   Print Labels from the COURSES File

Assume that you are preparing labels for the notebooks you use in your courses. Use the COURSES file to print labels that contain the number and name of the course so that they are centered on different lines separated by two blank lines. Use a 1 7/16 × 5 × 1 label size.

▼ QUESTIONS

1. What steps do you follow to display the labels design screen?
2. List and briefly describe the steps you follow to design a label.
3. How do you select fields and text in the label box? How do you copy or move it?
4. Why do you save a label design?

▼ CONCEPTS

Most businesspeople do not actually use the database file itself. Generally, they use reports created from part of the information stored in the file. The file might contain information about all aspects of the business. Reports are then designed to organize specific information needed by different people such as the sales manager, the president, or the finance department. Each report provides only the information needed by those it is printed for. Reports are not always complicated. For example, checks prepared on computers are reports. Reports consist of selected fields from selected records.

When you create most reports with dBASE, you have to picture them as consisting of bands (Figure 35). Each band contains a specific type of information. Several bands are automatically included:

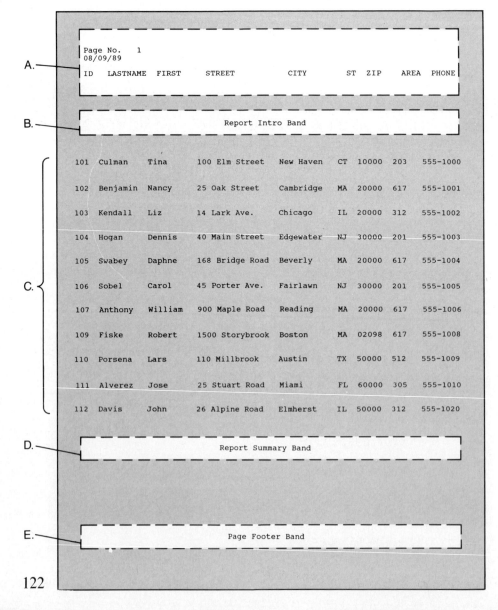

FIGURE 35 A Report's Bands. A printed report consists of a series of bands. Each band contains a specific type of information.
A. The Page Header Band
B. The Report Intro Band
C. The Detail Band
D. The Report Summary Band
E. The Page Footer Band

- The Page Header Band is where you enter information that you want to print as a header on each page of the report.
- The Report Intro is where you enter data that you want to begin the report. This can be comments, a memo, or fields.
- The Detail Band is where field name templates are inserted to refer to data in the database.
- The Report Summary Band is where you enter concluding remarks or calculate totals.
- The Page Footer Band is where you enter information that you want to print as a footer on each page of the report.

To create a report format, you highlight ⟨*create*⟩ on the Control Center's Reports panel, and then press Enter. This displays the reports design screen with the Layout menu automatically pulled down (Figure 36). From this menu, you can select *Quick layouts* to use one of the three predefined report formats:

- A Column layout is the same as the quick report format that you print when you press SHIFT-F9 (Figure 37). Like the printout in Figure 35, the screen is divided into bands. Each band has a heading below which is the shaded layout surface onto which you can enter data.
- A Form layout is like the Edit screen.
- A Mailmerge layout allows you to enter form letters so that data are inserted automatically from the database.

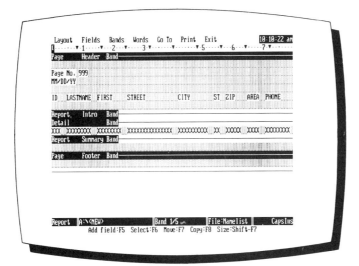

FIGURE 36 The Reports Design Screen and Layout Menu. When you select ⟨*create*⟩ from the Reports panel, the reports design screen is displayed with the Layout menu automatically pulled down.

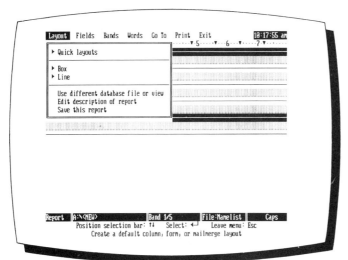

FIGURE 37 The Column Report Design Screen. The report design screen lists menu choices you use to define a report format.

123

WORD WRAP AND LAYOUT MODES

Once you select your report format, you can use it as is to print reports or you can customize it. You customize a report format on the reports design screen using two work surfaces, word wrap and layout:

- A word wrap work surface acts just like a word processor. With this mode you can enter explanatory notes or even write complete form letters for mail merge. Word wrap mode is used to enter text into labels and reports or when merge printing letters. When you enter text into a word wrap band, text wraps to a new line when it reaches the right margin. When preparing a report, you can use the choice on the Word menu to specify that any band be a word wrap band, and then use this mode to enter text into it. A word wrap band does not have the shaded background of other bands, and a cursor indicates where the next character you type will appear.
- A layout work surface is used to place fields, move them about, and add boxes and lines. You can enter text in layout bands, but lines don't wrap. If you try to enter text past the right margin, the computer beeps. Margin settings are used only to align fields and text using the *Position* choice on the Words menu. Moreover, layout surfaces initially comprise only blanks, which appear shaded on your screen. As you enter text or fields, these blanks are replaced with characters or templates. To restore the blanks, you delete the characters, including spaces that you enter with SPACEBAR.

When working on either of these surfaces, you have access to the editing commands described in Table 33 and the menu choices on the Fields (Table 31), Bands (Table 36), Words (Table 34), Go To (Table 14), and Print (Table 32) menus.

GROUP BANDS

If you want to calculate subtotals in a report, or use functions to analyze parts of the data, you can create group bands (Figure 38). You can enter these group bands into the page header band, the report intro band, or an existing group intro band above the detail band. A group can be defined by any of the following qualities:

- Record count is used to group a set number of records together. For example, you can specify that every fifty records form a group.
- Field value starts a new group based on the value in a specified field. When the value changes, so does the group. For example, you can index records by state, and then specify that the state value be used to group the records. You can then calculate subtotals by state.
- Expression starts the new group based on a field name, operator, or function. You can press SHIFT-F1 to display a list to choose from.

TABLE 33 Word Wrap Editing Commands

To	Press
Turn insert mode on and off	INS
You can press INS to switch between insert and typeover modes. When insert is on, the status bar displays *Ins,* and the cursor appears thicker than it does in typeover mode.	
Start a new paragraph	ENTER
• On a word wrap work surface, pressing ENTER ends a line and moves the cursor down one line and back to the left margin.	
• On a layout work surface, pressing ENTER has different results when insert is on or off. If insert is off, pressing ENTER moves the cursor down one line and back to the left margin without affecting any text. If insert is on, pressing ENTER inserts a blank line. If there is text or fields to the right of the cursor, it moves down one line. You can also press CTRL-N or pull down the Words menu and select *Add line* to insert a blank line.	
Select text	F6, then arrow keys, ENTER
Move a selected block to the cursor's position	F7
Copy a selected block to the cursor's position	F8
Delete the character above the cursor	DEL
Delete the character to the left of the cursor	BACKSPACE
Delete from the cursor to the beginning of the next word	CTRL-T
Delete the previous word	CTRL-BACKSPACE
Delete the current line	CTRL-Y

TABLE 34 The Words Menu

Menu Choice	Description
Style	Selects format for selected text or field. You can choose normal, bold, underline, italic, superscript, or subscript.
Display	Assigns colors to selected formatted text on the screen.
Position	Aligns text with the margins, left, right, or centered. The material affected depends on the cursor's position. • If only one character is selected when you use this command, the entire line is aligned. • If more than one character or field is selected, the selected block is aligned relative to other text and fields to the left and right.

TABLE 34 **(continued)**

Menu Choice	Description
Modify ruler	Moves the cursor to the ruler line so that you can change margins or tab stops. • To move the cursor, press SPACEBAR, CTRL-→ or CTRL-←, TAB or BACKTAB, END or HOME. • To specify a margin at the cursor's position, press [(left margin) or] (right margin). • To specify an indent, press #. (If you change the left margin, the indent automatically changes.) • To reset the left margin and indent to their original positions, press 0 (zero). • To set a tab at the cursor's position, press !. • To set tabs at evenly spaced intervals, press = and the prompt reads *Number of spaces:*. Type the number of spaces you want between tab stops, and then press ENTER. • To delete a tab stop at the cursor's position, press DEL. To delete one to the left of the cursor, press BACKSPACE. • To save your changes, press CTRL-END. To abandon them, press ESC.
Hide ruler	Hides and displays the ruler.
Enable automatic indent	Sets (in word wrap bands) the program so that pressing TAB or BACKTAB automatically resets the left margin so that all text aligns with the new setting until it is changed by pressing TAB or BACKTAB again.
Add line	Inserts a new line following the line with the cursor.
Remove line	Removes the current line.
Insert page break	Inserts a page break into word wrap text.
Write/read text file	Saves and retrieves text files to and from the disk.

The field value and expression procedures work only with indexed files because the records that are affected must be together in the file. If you group on state, and the file is not indexed by state, your report will not print correctly.

A group band contains two parts, the group's intro band and the group's summary band:

• The group's intro band contains information that is printed in each group followed by information that changes. For example, you can have State: printed in each group followed by the state in that group, for example, State: CA.

• The group's summary band is used to enter summary functions that calculate data in fields in the group. You can use functions that calculate averages, counts, maximums, minimums, sums, standard deviations, and variance.

Group bands work only with files that are sorted or indexed on the field value or expression. If a file is not sorted or indexed on the correct field, the records are not grouped together, so your report will not show them grouped correctly.

```
Page No. 1
08/08/89
ID   LASTNAME FIRST  STREET         CITY       ST ZIP   AREA PHONE


This set of records is for the state of CT
101  Culman    Tina   100 Elm Street  New Haven  CT 10000 203  555-1000
State: CT has 1 record(s)

This set of records is for the state of FL
111  Alverez   Jose   25 Stuart Road  Miami      FL 60000 305  555-1010
State: FL has 1 record(s)

This set of records is for the state of IL
112  Davis     John   26 Alpine Road  Elmherst   IL 50000 312  555-1020
103  Kendall   Liz    14 Lark Ave.    Chicago    IL 20000 312  555-1002
State: IL has 2 record(s)

This set of records is for the state of MA
107  Anthony   William 900 Maple Road Reading    MA 20000 617  555-1006
102  Benjamin  Nancy  25 Oak Street   Cambridge  MA 20000 617  555-1001
109  Fiske     Robert 1500 Storybrook Boston     MA 02098 617  555-1008
105  Swabey    Daphne 168 Bridge Road Beverly    MA 20000 617  555-1004
State: MA has 4 record(s)

This set of records is for the state of NJ
104  Hogan     Dennis 40 Main Street  Edgewater  NJ 30000 201  555-1003
106  Sobel     Carol  45 Porter Ave.  Fairlawn   NJ 30000 201  555-1005
State: NJ has 2 record(s)

This set of records is for the state of TX
110  Porsena   Lars   110 Millbrook   Austin     TX 50000 512  555-1009
State: TX has 1 record(s)
```

FIGURE 38   Group Bands.   A group band is used to group records based on the information contained in a specific field. You can also add summary functions that total your records for each group or to perform other calculation that help you analyze your data. Here, a group band has been used to group records by state. A count summary function has been used to count the records in each group.

▼ PROCEDURES

This section describes the procedures that you follow to:

- Print a report
- Add or modify bands
- Save a report format

To Display the Reports Design Screen

1. Open the database file you want to create a report for.
2. Press TAB to move the highlight to the Reports panel.
3. Highlight ⟨*create*⟩, and then press ENTER to display the reports design screen (Figure 39). The Layout menu is pulled down.
4. Press Q for *Quick layouts* to display a submenu.
5. Choose any of the layouts described in Table 35.

127

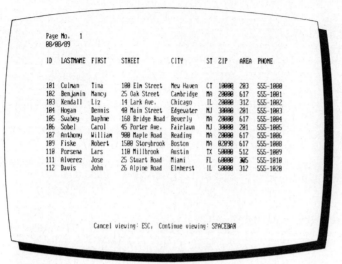

FIGURE 39 The NAMELIST Report Displayed on the Screen. Here, the report is shown displayed on the screen for checking before printing.

TABLE 35 The Layout Menu

Menu Choice	Description
Quick layouts	Displays a submenu listing three predefined report formats that you can use as is or modify.
	• *Column layout* is the same as the quick report format that you print when you press SHIFT-F9 (Figure 36).
	• *Form layout* is like the Edit screen.
	• *Mailmerge layout* allows you to enter form letters so that data are inserted automatically from the database.
Box	Specifies if the box is to be printed with a single line, a double line, or any other character that you specify.
Line	(Same choices as for *Box.*)
Use different database file or view	Specifies that another database or view be used with the report format.
Edit description of report	Adds or edits a description of the report that is displayed on the current file description area of the Control Center when the file's name is highlighted in the Reports panel.
Save this report	Saves the report format so that you can use it again.

To Add or Modify a Band

1. Position the cursor in the band.
2. Press ALT-B to pull down the Bands menu.
3. Make any of the selections described in Table 36.

To Save a Report Format

1. Press ALT-L to pull down the Layout menu. (You can select the *Edit description of this report* to add a description before saving.)
2. Press S for *Save this report,* and the prompt reads *Save as:.*
3. Type the name of the label, and then press ENTER.

TABLE 36   The Bands Menu

Menu Choice	Description
Add a group band	Inserts a group band within the page header band, the report intro band, or an existing group intro band. You can create groups based on field values, expressions, or record counts.
Remove group	Removes the current group, including the group intro band and group summary band. You can also delete a group by moving the highlight to its border and then pressing DEL.
Modify group	Changes the value used to make up the current group.
Group intro on each page	Specifies (when a group prints on more than one page) if the group intro is printed on the second and subsequent pages.
Open all bands	Opens all bands so that you can see what they contain.
Begin band on new page	Specifies if each new grouping for the group band starts on a new page when the current grouping value changes.
Word wrap band	Changes a layout band to a word wrap band and vice versa.
Text pitch for band	Sets the character pitch used to print data in the band. This setting takes precedence over the same setting on the Print menu.
Quality print for band	Sets the print quality used to print data in the band. This setting takes precedence over the same setting on the Print menu.
Spacing of lines for band	Sets the spacing of lines in the band. This setting takes precedence over the same setting on the Print menu.
Page heading in report intro	Prints (when set to *NO*) an introductory page that does not display the page header and footer bands. You enter a hard page break below the text to appear on this page with the *Insert page break* command on the Words menu.

To Print the Report

1. Press ALT-P to pull down the Print menu.
2. Make any of the selections described in Table 32.
3. Press B for *Begin printing.*

▼TIPS

➤ **After saving a report format, you can modify the design** using the same procedures you used to create it. To display the reports design screen, highlight the file's name on the Control Center. Press SHIFT-F2 or press ENTER and then select *Modify layout* from the submenu that appears. If the report is listed below the line in the panel, you are asked if you want to use the current view or the file the report was initially created for. If you specify the current view, the report can be used to print a report for the current database. If you specify the original file, that file is opened.

➤ **You cannot enter the double quotation mark (") in layout surfaces or word bands.** If you do, the computer will beep. Use the single quotation marks (') instead.

➤ **Three of the menus on the reports design screen are described in other topics.** The Fields menu is described in Table 31 (Topic 12), the Go To menu is described in Table 15 (Topic 6), and the Print menu is described in Table 32 (Topic 12).

TUTORIAL 13A
Printing a Report from the NAMELIST File

In this tutorial, you print a report for the NAMELIST file.

Step 1   **Open the NAMELIST File.** Before proceeding:

1. Load dBASE so that the Control Center is displayed.
2. Insert your data disk into drive A, and then change the default drive to drive A. (The current file and description section of the Control Center should read *A:\MYFILES.CAT.*)
3. Open the NAMELIST database so that its name is above the ruled line in the Control Center's Data panel.

Step 2   **Display the Reports Design Screen.** To begin, display the reports design screen so that you can lay out a report in column format.

To display the reports design screen

Press   TAB to move the highlight to the Reports panel, highlight ⟨*create*⟩, and then press ENTER. The Layout menu is automatically pulled down

Press   Q for *Quick layouts* to display a submenu

Press   C for *Column layout*

Result.   The reports design screen is displayed (Figure 36).

Step 3   **Open all Bands.** Now, open all bands so that you can see what is inside them.

To open all bands

Press   ALT-B to pull down the Bands menu

Press   O for *Open all bands*

Result.   All bands open. The shading between the band headings is the layout work surface. Experiment with pressing F4 and F3 to move the cursor between the band headings.

Step 4   **Display the Report on the Screen.** Let's preview the results by displaying the report on the screen.

To display a report on the screen

Press   ALT-P to pull down the Print menu

Press   V for *View report on screen*

Result.   The drive spins, and in a moment, the report is displayed on the screen (Figure 36). Press ESC and then press any key to return to the reports design screen.

Step 5   **Save the Report Format.** Now, save the report format and return to the Control Center.

To save the report format

Press   ALT-L to pull down the Layout menu

Press   S for *Save this report,* and the prompt reads *Save as:*

Type   **REPORT1** and then press ENTER

Result.   The drive spins as the report format is saved.

Step 6   **Print Out the Report.** Now, let's print the report.

To print the report
- Press   ALT-P to pull down the Print menu
- Press   B for *Begin printing*

Result.   The report prints out on your printer.

Step 7   **Sort the Report.** When you are printing reports, you can display the queries design screen at any time to filter or sort records. Let's sort the file in ascending order by last name, and then print the report.

To sort the report
- Press   SHIFT-F2 to display the queries design screen
- Press   TAB to move the cursor to the *LASTNAME* field
- Press   ALT-F to pull down the Fields menu
- Press   S for *Sort on this field* to display a submenu
- Highlight   *Ascending ASCII,* and then press ENTER

To print the report
- Press   SHIFT-F2 to process the query and return to the reports design screen
- Press   ALT-P to pull down the Print menu
- Press   B for *Begin printing*

Result.   The report prints out sorted by last name in ascending order. Press ALT-E to pull down the Exit menu, and then press A for *Abandon changes and exit.* The prompt reads *Query design has been changed. Do you want to save it?.* Press N.

Step 8   **Continue or Quit.** You have now completed this tutorial. Either continue with the next tutorial or quit the program.

TUTORIAL 13B
Adding a Group Band

In this tutorial, you revise the report format you saved in Tutorial 13A to add a group band that calculates subtotals and totals.

Step 1   **Open the NAMELIST File.** Before proceeding:

1. Load dBASE so that the Control Center is displayed.
2. Insert your data disk into drive A, and then change the default drive to drive A. (The current file and description section of the Control Center should read *A:\MYFILES.CAT.*)
3. Open the NAMELIST database so that its name is above the ruled line in the Control Center's Data panel.

Step 2   **Display the Reports Design Screen.** To begin, display the reports design screen so that you can lay out a report in column format.

131

To display the reports design screen

Press	TAB to move the highlight to the Reports panel, highlight *REPORT1,* and then press ENTER to display a submenu
Press	M for *Modify layout*

Result. The reports design screen is displayed (Figure 36).

Step 3 **Add a Group Band.** Now, add a group band.

To add a group band

Move	the cursor to the line above the *Report Intro Band* heading (The status bar reads *Line:5 Col:0.*)
Press	ALT-B to pull down the Bands menu
Press	A for *Add a group band* to display a submenu
Press	F for *Field value* to display a list of fields
Highlight	*ST,* and then press ENTER

Result. A group intro and summary band both appear on the screen.

Step 4 **Sort and Print Out the File.** Since you specified that the records be grouped by state, you have to either index or sort the file on that field. Let's sort it, and then print the file.

To sort the file

Press	SHIFT-F2 to display the queries design screen
Press	TAB to move the cursor to the *ST* field
Press	ALT-F to pull down the Fields menu
Press	S for *Sort on this field* to display a submenu
Highlight	*Ascending ASCII,* and then press ENTER

To print the report

Press	SHIFT-F2 to process the query and return to the reports design screen
Press	ALT-P to pull down the Print menu
Press	B for *Begin printing*

Result. The report prints out with all the records grouped together by state.

Step 5 **Add a Group Introduction and Summary.** Let's add a group introduction and summary.

To add a group introduction

Move	the cursor to the leftmost column in the shaded area below the *Group 1 Intro Band* heading
Type	**This group of records is for the state of**
Press	→ to move the cursor two spaces to the right
Press	ALT-F to pull down the Fields menu
Press	A for *Add field* to display a list of fields to choose from
Highlight	*ST,* and then press ENTER to display a submenu
Press	CTRL-END to save the settings

To add a group summary

Move	the cursor to the leftmost column in the shaded area below the *Group 1 Summary Band* heading
Type	**State:**
Press	→ to move the cursor two spaces to the right
Press	ALT-F to pull down the Fields menu
Press	A for *Add field* to display a list of fields to choose from
Highlight	*ST,* and then press ENTER
Press	CTRL-END to save the settings

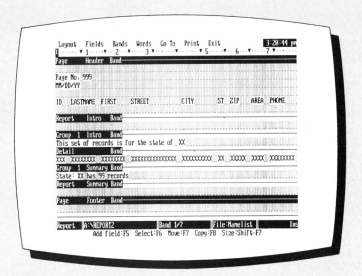

FIGURE 40 The NAMELIST Report Design with a Group Band. When you are finished adding the group band, your report format should look like this.

Result. Your design screen should look like Figure 40 (without the *has 99 records* entry in the *Group 1 Summary Band*).

Step 6 **Print Out the File.** Now, print the file.

To print the report

| Press | ALT-P to pull down the Print menu |
| Press | B for *Begin printing* |

Result. The report prints out with introductions and summaries for each group.

Step 7 **Add a Summary Function.** Let's add a summary function that indicates the number of records in each group.

To add a summary function

Move	the cursor to the shaded area below the *Group 1 Summary Band heading*
Press	END to move the cursor to the end of the current entry
Press	→ to move the cursor one space to the right
Type	**has**
Press	→ to move the cursor one space to the right
Press	ALT-F to pull down the Fields menu
Press	A for *Add field* to display a list of fields to choose from
Highlight	*Count* in the *SUMMARY* column, and then press ENTER
Press	T for *Template* to display a submenu
Press	BACKSPACE to delete all but two 9s, and then press ENTER to display a submenu
Press	CTRL-END to save the settings
Press	→ to move the cursor one space to the right
Type	**record(s)**

Result. Your design screen should now look exactly like Figure 40.

Step 8 **Print Out the File.** Now, print the file.

To print the report

| Press | ALT-P to pull down the Print menu |
| Press | B for *Begin printing* |

Result. The report prints out with introductions and summaries for each group.

133

Step 9 **Save the Report Format and Exit.** Let's save this revised report format under a new name.

To save the report under a new name

Press ALT-L to pull down the Layout menu
Press S for *Save this report,* and the prompt reads *Save as: A:\RE-PORT1.FRM*
Press HOME and then press CTRL-Y to delete the current entry
Type **REPORT2** and then press ENTER to save the report

To return to the Control Center

Press ALT-E to pull down the Exit menu
Press A for *Abandon changes and exit.* The prompt reads *Query design has been changed. Do you want to save it?.* Press N

Result. The Control Center reappears, and the new report format is listed.

Step 10 **Continue or Quit.** You have now completed this tutorial. Either continue with the next tutorial or quit the program.

▼EXERCISES

EXERCISE 13A   Change Print Settings

Open the NAMELIST file, and then modify the REPORT2 report format. Use the Print menu choices to change the text pitch and the offset from left settings. Experiment with the settings, and when you find ones you like, save them to a print form named MYPRINT.

EXERCISE 13B   Generate a Report for the PLACEST File

Prepare a report for the PLACEST file so that the records are sorted by per capita income in 1985. Table 12 describes the fields in the file.

▼QUESTIONS

1. What is a report?
2. What are bands? List and briefly describe the ones that are displayed and printed automatically.
3. What is the purpose of the *Quick layouts* choice on the Layout menu? What choices does this command offer you? How do they differ?
4. What is a word wrap work surface? A layout work surface? What do you use each for?
5. What is the purpose of a group band? What must be done to the file to make one print correctly?

CONCEPTS

If you have two or more files with a common field, you can link them. This procedure constructs a database view that shows fields from both files, provided both files have the same value in a specified common field. Normally, you link files only when one of them has unique data in the linked fields. Since every possible combination is linked, strange combinations will result if neither file has unique data.

FIGURE 41 Linking Files. Here, the NAMELIST and AMOUNTS files contain a common ID field (a) that can be used to link them into a new table (c). All records that fail to have the same value in the common field are deleted from the new table.

ID	LASTNAME	FIRST	STREET	CITY	ST	ZIP	AREA	PHONE
101	Culman	Tina	100 Elm Street	New Haven	CT	10000	203	555-1000
102	Benjamin	Nancy	25 Oak Street	Cambridge	MA	20000	617	555-1001
103	Kendall	Liz	14 Lark Ave.	Chicago	IL	20000	312	555-1002
104	Hogan	Dennis	40 Main Street	Edgewater	NJ	30000	201	555-1003
105	Swabey	Daphne	168 Bridge Road	Beverly	MA	20000	617	555-1004
106	Sobel	Carol	45 Porter Ave.	Fairlawn	NJ	30000	201	555-1005
107	Anthony	William	900 Maple Road	Reading	MA	20000	617	555-1006
109	Fiske	Robert	1500 Storybrook	Boston	MA	02098	617	555-1008
110	Porsena	Lars	110 Millbrook	Austin	TX	50000	512	555-1009
111	Alverez	Jose	25 Stuart Road	Miami	FL	60000	305	555-1010
112	Davis	John	26 Alpine Road	Elmherst	IL	50000	312	555-1020

A. The NAMELIST Database File

ID	DATE	AMOUNT
101	6/8/90	11.00
102	6/9/90	16.50
103	6/10/90	38.50
104	6/11/90	25.00
105	6/12/90	30.00
106	6/13/90	50.00
107	6/14/90	15.00
109	6/16/90	18.00
110	6/17/90	43.00
111	6/18/90	61.00
112	6/19/90	20.00

B. The AMOUNTS Database file

ID	LASTNAME	FIRST	STREET	CITY	ST	ZIP	AREA	PHONE	DATE	AMOUNT
101	Culman	Tina	100 Elm Street	New Haven	CT	10000	203	555-1000	6/8/90	11.00
102	Benjamin	Nancy	25 Oak Street	Cambridge	MA	20000	617	555-1001	6/9/90	16.50
103	Kendall	Liz	14 Lark Ave.	Chicago	IL	20000	312	555-1002	6/10/90	38.50
104	Hogan	Dennis	40 Main Street	Edgewater	NJ	30000	201	555-1003	6/11/90	25.00
105	Swabey	Daphne	168 Bridge Road	Beverly	MA	20000	617	555-1004	6/12/90	30.00
106	Sobel	Carol	45 Porter Ave.	Fairlawn	NJ	30000	201	555-1005	6/13/90	50.00
107	Anthony	William	900 Maple Road	Reading	MA	20000	617	555-1006	6/14/90	15.00
109	Fiske	Robert	1500 Storybrook	Boston	MA	02098	617	555-1008	6/16/90	18.00
110	Porsena	Lars	110 Millbrook	Austin	TX	50000	512	555-1009	6/17/90	43.00
111	Alverez	Jose	25 Stuart Road	Miami	FL	60000	305	555-1010	6/18/90	61.00
112	Davis	John	26 Alpine Road	Elmherst	IL	50000	312	555-1020	6/19/90	20.00

C. The Files Linked on the ID
Field to Creat a New View

After linking files, you can specify which fields are to be included in the view and query the linked files to save them into a new file (Figure 41). For example, you can link the customer names in one file with the amounts they owe in another to create a new table. At the end of each month, the AMOUNTS file can be linked with the NAMELIST file to prepare a complete file from which reports and bills can be prepared. When the two files are linked, the customer's ID number, which appears in both files, is used as the identifying, or key, field.

To link files, you display the queries design screen for one of the files. You then use the Layout menu to add a new file, and its file skeleton appears on the screen. There are then two ways to link the two files:

- Enter an example variable (any eight-character name) into the same field in each file skeleton.
- Use the *Create link by pointing* choice on the Layout menu to automatically enter the example variable in the fields that you point to.

▼PROCEDURES

This section describes the procedures that you follow to:

- Link database files
- Add and remove fields from the view
- Save linked files into a new file

To Link Database Files

1. Open the first database file that you want to link to another.
2. Press TAB to move the highlight to the Queries panel, highlight ⟨*create*⟩, and then press ENTER.
3. Press ALT-L to pull down the Layout menu, and then press A for *Add file to query* to display a list of files in the catalog.
4. Highlight the other file you want to link, and then press ENTER.
5. Press TAB to move the highlight to the common field, and then press ALT-L to pull down the Layout menu.
6. Press C for *Create link by pointing* to enter the first example variable.
7. Press F3 to move the cursor to the next file skeleton, point to the field you want to link in that file, and then press ENTER (Figure 42).

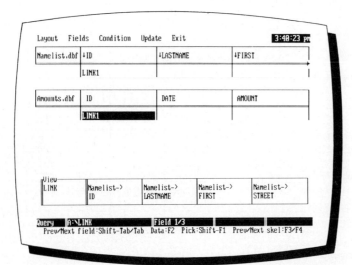

FIGURE 42 The Queries Design Screen with Linked Files. When you enter the links, your screen should look like this.

To Add or Remove Fields

1. Link two or more files.
2. Press TAB to move to the fields to be added to or removed from the view, and then press F5.

To Create a New File from Linked Files

1. Link two or more files.
2. Specify the fields to be included in the view.
3. Press ALT-L to pull down the Layout menu.
4. Press W for *Write this view as database file,* and the prompt reads *Enter filename:.*
5. Type the name of the file you want to save the combined fields into, and then press ENTER.
6. Either press ALT-E to pull down the Exit menu, and then press S for *Save changes and exit.* The prompt reads *Save as:.* Type the name of the query, and then press ENTER.

   Or press ALT-E to pull down the Exit menu, and then press A for *Abandon changes and exit.* The prompt reads *Are you sure you want to abandon operation?.* Press Y.

TUTORIAL 14A
Linking the NAMELIST and AMOUNTS Files

In this tutorial, you link the NAMELIST and AMOUNTS files to form two new files named NEWFILE1 and NEWFILE2.

Step 1 **Open the NAMELIST File.** Before proceeding:

1. Load dBASE so that the Control Center is displayed.
2. Insert your data disk into drive A, and then change the default drive to drive A. (The current file and description section of the Control Center should read *A:\MYFILES.CAT.*)
3. Open the NAMELIST database so that its name is above the ruled line in the Control Center's Data panel.

Step 2 **Link Files.** The first step in combining two files is to link them.

To link files

Press	TAB to move the highlight to the Queries panel, highlight ⟨*create*⟩, and then press ENTER
Press	ALT-L to pull down the Layout menu
Press	A for *Add file to query* to display a list of files in the catalog
Highlight	*AMOUNTS.DBF,* and then press ENTER
Press	TAB to move to the *ID* field for *Amounts.dbf*
Press	ALT-L to pull down the Layout menu
Press	C for *Create link by pointing.* (*LINK1* is displayed in the *ID* field.)
Press	F3 to move the highlight to the Namelist.dbf field on the file skeleton
Press	TAB to move to the *ID* field for *Namelist.dbf,* and then press ENTER

To add fields

Press	F4 to move the highlight to the Amounts.dbf field on the file skeleton
Press	TAB to move the highlight to the *DATE* field, and then press F5
Press	TAB to move the highlight to the *AMOUNT* field, and then press F5

Result. The query is complete (Figure 42).

Step 3 **Display the Linked Files.** Once a link is established, and the fields to appear in the view are selected, you can display the resulting file.

To display the file

Press	F2 to process the query

Result. The linked files are displayed on the screen (Figure 43). Press TAB to scroll the screen horizontally so that you can see the AMOUNT field.

Step 4 **Join Complete Files.** Now let's save the linked files to a new file.

To join the files into a new file

Press	SHIFT-F2 to display the queries design screen
Press	ALT-L to pull down the Layout menu
Press	W for *Write this view as database file,* and the prompt reads *Enter filename:*
Type	**NEWFILE1** and then press ENTER

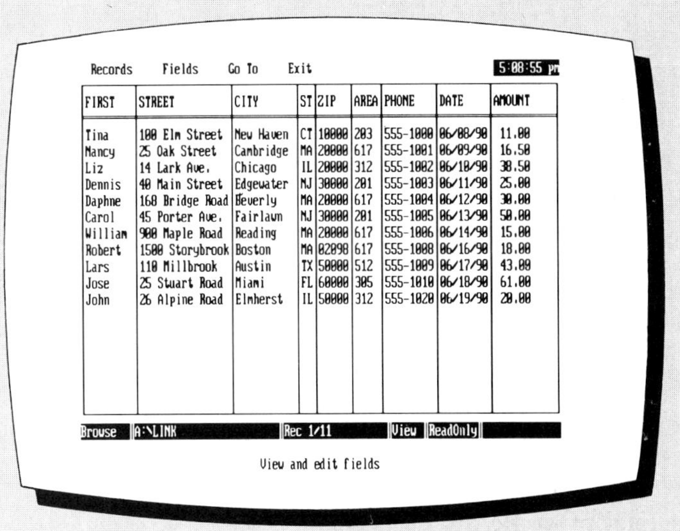

FIRST	STREET	CITY	ST	ZIP	AREA	PHONE	DATE	AMOUNT
Tina	100 Elm Street	New Haven	CT	10000	203	555-1000	06/08/90	11.00
Nancy	25 Oak Street	Cambridge	MA	20000	617	555-1001	06/09/90	16.50
Liz	14 Lark Ave.	Chicago	IL	20000	312	555-1002	06/10/90	30.50
Dennis	40 Main Street	Edgewater	NJ	30000	201	555-1003	06/11/90	25.00
Daphne	168 Bridge Road	Beverly	MA	20000	617	555-1004	06/12/90	30.00
Carol	45 Porter Ave.	Fairlawn	NJ	30000	201	555-1005	06/13/90	50.00
William	900 Maple Road	Reading	MA	20000	617	555-1006	06/14/90	15.00
Robert	1500 Storybrook	Boston	MA	02090	617	555-1008	06/16/90	18.00
Lars	110 Millbrook	Austin	TX	50000	512	555-1009	06/17/90	43.09
Jose	25 Stuart Road	Miami	FL	60000	305	555-1010	06/18/90	61.00
John	26 Alpine Road	Elmherst	IL	50000	312	555-1020	06/19/90	20.00

FIGURE 43 The Linked Files. When you display the linked files, your screen should look like this when you scroll the AMOUNT field into view.

To return to the Control Center

Press ALT-E to pull down the Exit menu
Press S for *Save changes and exit,* and the prompt reads *Save as:*
Type **LINK** and then press ENTER

Result. The Control Center reappears. The joined file, NEWFILE1, is listed in the Data panel, and the query, LINK, is listed in the Queries panel.

Step 5 Display the New File. Now, display the new file.

To display the new file

Press TAB to move the highlight to the Data panel
Highlight *NEWFILE1,* and then press F2

Result. The new file appears on the screen and looks just like the original NAMELIST file. But the two fields combined from the AMOUNTS file are at the right side of the screen. Press END to pan the file to the left. The new database file now contains DATE and AMOUNT fields. Press HOME to pan the file to the right. Press ALT-E to pull down the Exit menu, and then press E for *Exit* to return to the Control Center.

Step 6 Print Out the Records. Make a printout of the records in the database file. Before proceeding, be sure that the printer is ready.

To print out the records

Press SHIFT-F9 to display a submenu
Press B for *Begin printing*

Result. The records print out.

Step 7 Remove Selected Fields from the View. When you link two files, you need not combine all the fields. You can remove fields from the view so that they are not included in the new database file. For example, suppose you want to know the names and phone numbers of people who have outstanding charges so that you can call them to discuss the date and amount of their charge.

To link the fields into a new file

Press TAB to move the highlight to the Queries panel
Highlight *LINK*, and then press ENTER to display a submenu
Press M for *Modify View* to display the queries design screen

Result. Use F3, F4, and TAB to move the highlight to the following fields on the file skeleton, and then press F5 to remove them from the view, *ID, STREET, CITY, ST,* and *ZIP.*

Step 8 **Display the New File.** Now, display the new file.

To display the new file

Press   F2

Result. The new file contains the first and last names and phone numbers from the NAMELIST file and the amounts from the AMOUNTS file.

Step 9 **Join the Remaining Fields.** Now, join the fields that remain in the view to a new file.

To join the files into a new file

Press   SHIFT-F2 to display the queries design screen
Press   ALT-L to pull down the Layout menu
Press   W for *Write this view as database file,* and the prompt reads *Enter filename:.* (If an entry exists in the box, press BACKSPACE until it is deleted.)
Type   **NEWFILE2** and then press ENTER

To return to the Control Center

Press   ALT-E to pull down the Exit menu
Press   S for *Save changes and exit*

Result. The Control Center reappears, and the joined file, NEWFILE2, is listed in the Data panel.

Step 10 **Display the New File.** Now, display the new file.

To display the new file

Press   TAB to move the highlight to the Data panel
Highlight   *NEWFILE2,* and then press F2

Result. The new file appears on the screen and contains only the fields that you did not remove from the view. Press ALT-E to pull down the Exit menu, and then press E for *Exit* to return to the Control Center.

Step 11 **Print Out the Records.** Make a printout of the records in the database file. Before proceeding, be sure that the printer is ready.

To print out the records

Press   SHIFT-F9 to display a submenu
Press   B for *Begin printing*

Result. The records print out.

Step 12 **Continue or Quit.** You have now completed this tutorial. Either continue with the next tutorial or quit the program.

▼QUESTIONS

1. What happens when you link files?
2. What two methods can you use to link files?
3. After linking files, what can you do with them?

▼ Projects

This part contains a project on analyzing census data. This project tests and builds on the skills you have developed while learning dBASE IV. Occasionally while completing this project, you may encounter problems and become confused. But don't fret, for that is precisely the point of completing it. You really learn programs when you encounter problems and solve them. When you do so, you add new techniques to your library of knowledge about the program. The next time you encounter the same problem, you will already know the solution or be able to devise an even better one. So don't become discouraged at any point. Look at the completion of this project as a challenge, one that you will overcome and gain from. When completing this project, keep the following points in mind:

- The project assumes that you have mastered the procedures discussed in the appropriate topics. Topics you need to understand before completing the project (other than the basic and obvious ones like entering, editing, saving, and printing) are listed in the "Background Required" section at the beginning of the project.
- The "Concepts" section is designed to give you the subject area information you need to complete the project.
- The "Steps" section gives you the sequence of steps that you should follow when completing the project. If you get to a step that you have not yet covered in class, you can save the database at that point and retrieve it later when you have covered the required topic.

PROJECT 1
Analyzing Census Data

▼ BACKGROUND REQUIRED

To complete this project, you must have completed the following topics:

- Topic 8   Sorting Records
- Topic 9   Indexing Records
- Topic 10   Querying a Database
- Topic 11   Using Relational Operators and Making Calculations
- Topic 13   Printing Reports

141

▼ PROJECT DESCRIPTION

The Bureau of the Census releases much of their census data on floppy disks. This data is widely used by statisticians and people in market research. In this project, you work with one of the many files supplied by the Bureau. This database contains a sample of data from the County and City Data Book 1988 (CCDB). The CCDB is a compendium of statistics from the Bureau of the Census and fifteen other national agencies. This database (Figure 1) includes the fields of information described in Table 1.

FIGURE 1   The Census Database.   This database file was prepared by the Bureau of the Census and gives some statistical data on the fifty states.

STATE	AREANAME	POP01080	POP01086	PCI01079	PCI01085	POP13086	PCI11085
19	IOWA	2913808	2851000	7136	10096	-2	42
11	DISTRICT OF COLUMBI	638432	626100	8959	13530	-2	51
54	WEST VIRGINIA	1950183	1919000	6142	8141	-2	33
26	MICHIGAN	9262044	9155000	7688	10902	-1	42
39	OHIO	10797604	10752000	7284	10371	0	42
42	PENNSYLVANIA	11864720	11889000	7075	10288	0	45
18	INDIANA	5490212	5504000	7141	9978	0	40
17	ILLINOIS	11427429	11548000	8064	11302	1	40
36	NEW YORK	17558165	17772000	7496	11765	1	57
25	MASSACHUSETTS	5737093	5832000	7457	12510	2	68
55	WISCONSIN	4705642	4785000	7241	10298	2	42
21	KENTUCKY	3660334	3727000	5973	8614	2	44
31	NEBRASKA	1569825	1598000	6934	10546	2	52
46	SOUTH DAKOTA	690768	707000	5696	8553	2	50
41	OREGON	2633156	2698000	7556	9925	3	31
09	CONNECTICUT	3107564	3189000	8511	14090	3	66
44	RHODE ISLAND	947154	975000	6897	10892	3	58
29	MISSOURI	4916762	5066000	6915	10283	3	49
27	MINNESOTA	4075970	4216000	7450	11186	3	50
34	NEW JERSEY	7365011	7620000	8127	13129	4	62
05	ARKANSAS	2286358	2372000	5613	8389	4	50
01	ALABAMA	3894025	4053000	5892	8681	4	47
20	KANSAS	2364236	2461000	7349	10684	4	45
28	MISSISSIPPI	2520770	2625000	5182	7483	4	44
30	MONTANA	786690	819000	6589	8781	4	33
38	NORTH DAKOTA	652717	680000	6417	9635	4	50
23	MAINE	1125043	1174000	5766	9042	4	57
47	TENNESSEE	4591036	4803000	6212	9290	5	50
24	MARYLAND	4216933	4463000	8293	12967	6	56
50	VERMONT	511456	541000	6177	9619	6	56
16	IDAHO	944127	1003000	6248	8567	6	37
10	DELAWARE	594338	633000	7449	11375	7	53
22	LOUISIANA	4206124	4501000	6425	8836	7	38
37	NORTH CAROLINA	5880416	6331000	6132	9517	8	55
53	WASHINGTON	4132353	4463000	8073	10866	8	35
56	WYOMING	469557	507000	7927	9782	8	23
45	SOUTH CAROLINA	3120737	3378000	5884	8890	8	51
51	VIRGINIA	5346797	5787000	7475	11894	8	59
40	OKLAHOMA	3025487	3305000	6854	9754	9	42
15	HAWAII	964691	1062000	7740	11003	10	42
33	NEW HAMPSHIRE	920610	1027000	6966	11659	12	67
13	GEORGIA	5462989	6104000	6380	10191	12	60
08	COLORADO	2889735	3267000	7998	11713	13	46
35	NEW MEXICO	1303303	1479000	6120	8814	14	44
06	CALIFORNIA	23667764	26981000	8294	11885	14	43
49	UTAH	1461037	1665000	6305	8535	14	35
48	TEXAS	14225512	16682000	7203	10373	17	44
04	ARIZONA	2716598	3244000	7042	10561	19	50
12	FLORIDA	9746959	11675000	7260	11271	20	55
32	NEVADA	800508	964000	8453	11200	20	33
02	ALASKA	401851	534000	10193	13650	33	34

TABLE 1   The Census Database

Field	Description
STATE	FIPS state code
AREANAME	Area name
POP01080	Population April 1, 1980
POP01086	Population July 1, 1986 (estimate)
PCI01079	Per capita income 1979
PCI01085	Per capita income 1985
POP13086	Population percent change 1980–1986
PCI11085	Per capita income, percent change 1979–1985

▼CONCEPTS

One of the key advantages of storing information in a database is that you can view the data in a variety of ways. Over the past few years, many studies and reports have discussed the shifts in the U.S. population between regions. Many of these studies have been based on the analysis of databases compiled by the U.S Bureau of the Census. These population statistics are gathered through house-to-house calls and are updated periodically to keep them current. The final results are used by the government to allocate seats in the U.S. House of Representatives and by businesses to project markets and locations of stores, factories, and offices.

▼STEPS

1. Add the PLACEST.DBF file on your *Resource Disk* to your MYFILES catalog if you have not done so already.
2. Make a printout the database's structure, and then compare the printout with the description of each field in Table 1.
3. Print out a quick report of the database. If all eight fields are not printed on the same page:
   • Use the *Control of Printer* option to change the text pitch to condensed or elite.
   • If changing pitch does not work, remove the following fields from the view since they are not used in this analysis: PCI01079 and PCI11085.
4. Compare each field's contents in the printout with their description in Table 1.

▼PROBLEMS

1. Assume you are assigned to an evaluation team that proposes new locations for retail stores. Top management has asked you to prepare an analysis that shows the fastest growing and the slowest growing states. To do so, they want you to use the population percent change in the period between 1980 and 1986 since those are the years with the most current statistics.
   • Begin by sorting the database into descending order using the POP13086 field, and then print out a quick report. What is the fastest growing state? What is the slowest? (Actually it is shrinking!)
   • Enter a query that displays only those states with a percent change greater than 10% OR less than 1%. (You do not enter decimal places in percent figures in this database; for example, to enter 10%, enter it as 10.) Process the query, and then print out a quick report. Based solely on this report,

143

what state would you recommend as the site for the first new store? What state would you recommend that the company reduce their investment in?

- Save the query as HILO1, and then return to the Control Center.

2. After looking at the initial report you prepared in Problem 1, management realizes that per capita income should be used as a criterion in selecting new sites. They ask you to prepare a new analysis using the per capita income in 1985 data.

- Open the PLACEST database, and then select the HILO1 query as the view.
- Sort the database into descending order using the PCIO1085 field, and then print out a quick report. Based solely on this report, what state would you recommend as the site for the first new store? What state would you recommend that the company reduce their investment in?
- Save the query as HILO2, and then return to the Control Center.

3. Management has accepted your proposal and would like a polished report for another meeting.

- Open the PLACEST database using the HILO2 query as a view. Then create a report using the *Column Layout* option and the following settings:
Set the right margin to 7½ inches.
In the Header Band, center the heading ANALYSIS OF NEW STORE LOCATIONS.
- Change the Report Intro Band to a word wrap band, and then enter the following description: "This analysis is based on the U.S. Bureau of the Census data from 1988."
- Enter your name into the Page Footer Band.
- Print out the report.
- Save the report under the name HILO2 and then return to the Control Center.

APPENDIX

Understanding DOS

Introduction

All applications programs that operate on a microcomputer require an operating system. Because the operating system coordinates activity between any applications program you run and the computer hardware, you must load the operating system into the computer's memory before you load an applications program. Most applications programs that you buy from publishers do not contain the operating system. To use these programs, you must first load the operating system from another disk, or copy the appropriate operating system program files to the applications program disk or your hard disk. This is necessary because the operating system may have been published by one company and the applications program by another. Even if the same company publishes both, they are not sure which version of their operating system you may be using, so they cannot anticipate which version to put on the disk.

When IBM developed the original IBM PC, they contracted the development of its operating system to Microsoft, which developed an operating system called MS-DOS (Microsoft Disk Operating System). The IBM PC version of this program was named PC-DOS. The PC-DOS version usually runs on IBM PC computers, and the MS-DOS version usually runs on compatibles made by manufacturers other than IBM. These two versions of the operating system are essentially identical in the way they work and the commands you use to operate them; usually they are interchangeable. Since the IBM PC set the standard for microcomputers, MS-DOS and PC-DOS are the most widely used operating systems.

As computers have evolved, so have operating systems. When major changes are made in the operating system, it is released as a new version. For example, DOS was initially released as version 1.0, and over the years, versions 2.0, 3.0, and 4.0 have been released. Minor changes also are introduced periodically. These are usually identified with numbers following the decimal point. For example, DOS is available in versions 3.0, 3.1, 3.2, 3.3, 4.0, and 4.01. Normally, programs that run on an early version will also run on a later version. This appendix discusses all versions of releases 3 and 4, so they are referred to as DOS 3 and DOS 4. The major difference between DOS 3 and 4 is the addition of the Shell to DOS 4. This version allows you to execute many of the most commonly used commands from these menus.

Note: All of the instructions in this appendix describe procedures that you follow when DOS's command prompt is displayed. If you are using DOS 3, the command prompt is displayed when you first load the operating system. (If you are working on a computer connected to a network, ask your instructor how you display this prompt.) However, if you are using DOS 4, your system may be set up to display the Shell. To follow the procedures described in this appendix, you must remove this Shell and display the command prompt. To do so, you have two choices:

- Press F3 from Start Programs to remove the Shell from memory. (You first have to press F3 if you are in the File System, or Esc if you are in the DOS Utilities' subgroup, to return to Start Programs.) You can also select *Exit Shell* from the Start Programs' Exit menu on the Action Bar. After using either command, type **DOSSHELL** and then press ENTER to return to the Shell if you want to display it again.
- Press SHIFT-F9 to leave the Shell in memory and load a second copy of the COMMAND.COM file. You can also select *Command Prompt* from the Start Programs' Main Group. These commands make it faster to return to the Shell when you want. To do so, type **EXIT** and then press ENTER. If you use this command, and there is not enough room in memory for the second copy of the COMMAND.COM program, an error message is displayed. Use the first procedure to display the command prompt.

1. UNDERSTANDING DISKS AND DISK DRIVES

When you work on a computer, the programs and files you work on are stored internally in the computer's random-access memory (RAM). This memory is a limited resource, yet it must serve many uses. Not only do you load different applications programs, you also create files for your own work, and there can be a lot of them. The computer's memory is not large enough to store all the programs, documents, and other computer-generated files you work on. Moreover, most memory will lose its data when you turn the computer off.

For these reasons, external storage (also called auxiliary or secondary storage) is provided. You use this storage to store programs and data that you are not using at the moment. Once data is stored externally, you can reload it into the computer's internal memory without having to rekeyboard it.

Computers usually use magnetic disks to store programs and files externally. Magnetic disks, and the devices used to store and retrieve data on them, fall into two major classes: floppy disks and disk drives and hard disk drives.

FLOPPY DISKS AND DISK DRIVES

Floppy disks for microcomputers come in two sizes: $5\frac{1}{4}$ and $3\frac{1}{2}$ inches. Each size works only with drives specifically designed to accept it. Though they vary in size, they have certain features in common (Figure 1):

1. A storage envelope protects $5\frac{1}{4}$-inch disks from scratches, dust, and fingerprints. Some envelopes are treated to eliminate the static buildup that attracts abrasive grit. These envelopes are not used on the better protected $3\frac{1}{2}$-inch disks.
2. A plastic outer covering protects the disk itself while allowing it to spin smoothly inside the jacket. $5\frac{1}{4}$-inch disks are protected by flexible plastic jackets, whereas $3\frac{1}{2}$-inch disks are mounted in a rigid plastic housing. The jacket or housing is permanently sealed and contains lubricants and cleaning agents that prolong the life of the disk.
3. The read/write slot in the jacket is where the disk drive's read/write head contacts the surface of the disk. This read/write head stores data on (writes) and retrieves data from (reads) the surface of the disk as the disk spins inside the drive. On $3\frac{1}{2}$-inch disks, the read/write slot is protected by a sliding metal cover called the shutter. When you insert the disk into the drive, this shutter

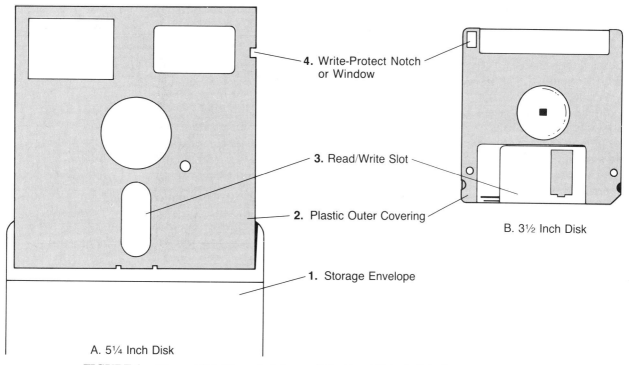

FIGURE 1 Floppy Disk Characteristics. $5\frac{1}{4}$-inch and $3\frac{1}{2}$-inch disks have many features in common.

is automatically pushed aside so that the read/write slot is exposed, and the drive can come in contact with the floppy disk within.

4. The write-protect notch or window allows you to write on a disk when it is not write-protected and prevents you from writing on the disk when it is (see the section "Write-Protect Your Disks"). A switch, or photoelectric circuit, inside the disk drive determines if the disk is write-protected. If it finds that it is, the switch disables the drive's ability to write information onto the disk.

If you were to remove the plastic jacket or housing of a floppy disk, you would find a round piece of plastic covered with a metallic oxide similar to the magnetic recording material used on audiotapes and videotapes. The round disk is sandwiched between two sheets of a soft, feltlike material, which is impregnated with a lubricant that protects the disk when it is spinning in the drive.

The floppy disk drive is the device that the floppy disk is inserted into so that you can store data to and retrieve data from it. The floppy disk drive has two parts you should be familiar with: the slot and the light (Figure 2).

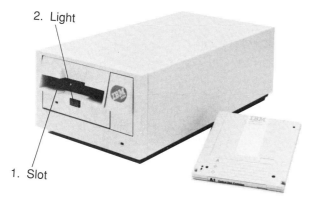

FIGURE 2 A Floppy Disk Drive. The floppy disk drive has two parts that you should be familiar with: the drive's slot and the drive's light. Here they are shown on a standalone drive, but most disk drives are built into the computer. *Courtesy of IBM Corporation*

Types of Floppy Disks

Since there is variation among computers, the disks you buy must be appropriate for the system you want to use them on. On every box of disks, and on most disk labels, are several terms that you should be familiar with. Knowing the number of sides, the density, and the sectors used by your system allows you to select and use the correct disks with your system.

SIDES

Disks are rated as single or double sided. Single-sided disks can store data on only one side of the disk. Double-sided disks can store data on both sides of the disk if your system's disk drive is capable of writing to both sides.

DENSITY

Data are stored on a disk on tracks, narrow concentric bands around the disk somewhat like the grooves on a 33⅓ record (al-though a record's groove is one continuous spiral and not a series of concentric circles). To store more data, the tracks are placed closer together. The spacing of these tracks is measured as tracks per inch (TPI). The maximum density that can be used to store data on a disk is indicated on the disk label and box.

- Single-density disks can store data on 24 TPI.
- Double-density disks can store data on 48 TPI or up to 360KB (KB stands for kilobytes).
- High-density disks (also called high-capacity or quad-density disks) can store data on 96 TPI.
- 3½-inch floppy disks can store 720KB or 1.44MB (MB stands for megabytes) on a double-sided disk. These smaller disks can store more data than the larger 5¼-inch disks because they can store data on 135 TPI.

1. The slot is where you insert a floppy disk into the drive (see the box "Inserting Floppy Disks" in Topic 1).
2. The light on the front of the drive goes on when the drive is operating. When the light is on, you should not open the door or eject a disk. Doing so can damage the disk and cause you to lose data. If you make a mistake and the drive spins when the door is open or without a disk inserted, do not close the door or insert a disk. In a few moments, a message will usually appear telling you the drive's door is open or no disk is in the drive. When the light goes out, close the door or insert a disk, and then follow the instructions displayed on the screen.

HARD DISK DRIVES

Hard disk drives (also called fixed disks or Winchester disk drives after their code name while being developed at IBM) were not commonly used with microcomputers until recently because of their high cost. But over the past few years, their cost has dropped dramatically. Lower cost and superior performance have made hard disk drives the first choice of serious computer users. Moreover, their storage capacity greatly reduces the number of disk "swaps" that have to be made when working with floppy disk drives. Since many operating systems and applications programs come on several floppy disks, this can save a great deal of time.

Instead of a floppy disk, hard disk drives use rigid metal platters to store data. This allows them to store data more densely. This increased density plus the number of platters greatly increases their storage capacity. Hard disk drives generally provide 10, 20, 40, or more megabytes of storage capacity, much more than a floppy disk. In addition, a hard disk drive spins at 3600 rpm, about ten times faster than a floppy disk drive, allowing data to be stored and retrieved faster.

In a floppy disk drive, the read/write heads are in contact with the disk. In a hard disk drive, they fly over its surface on a cushion of air with a space smaller than a piece of dust separating the head from the rapidly spinning disk. To imagine the small tolerances involved, picture an airplane flying at high speed $\frac{1}{2}$ inch above the ground without making contact. With the high speeds and small spaces involved, even a particle can cause the read/write head to come in contact with the disk's surface, creating a head crash. With the disk spinning at almost 60 mph, this can cause a lot of damage to the disk and the data stored on it.

When you use a hard disk drive, the read/write head is positioned on the disk where data is stored. If you are going to move your computer, use the park program (found on a disk that comes with your computer) to park the read/write head. This program moves the read/write head to a section of the disk that has no data, thus preventing the head from damaging data on the disk should it move. Even slightly jarring your computer may damage your files.

PROTECTING AND CARING FOR YOUR FILES AND DISKS

When you enter data into the computer, it is not stored permanently until you save it onto disks. But even then the data is not protected from loss or damage. No one ever heeds this advice until they loose important information and have to spend hours or days recreating it. Don't be like everyone else; follow these recommendations before you lose data.

Floppy Disk Storage

When you first start working on a microcomputer, the number of disks you work with is manageable. But before long, keeping disks filed in an orderly way can present quite a problem. Several disk filing systems have been developed, including plastic sleeves that can be inserted in three-ring binders, plastic cases, and sophisticated filing cabinets for large collections.

Labeling Your Disks

An unwritten rule among computer users is that an unlabeled disk contains no valuable files. People often do not take the time to check what files, if any, an unlabeled disk contains. Thus the first step when you use a disk is to label it. Always write the disk title, your name, the date, and the operating system version that you are using on the labels (Figure 3).

If you are using 5¼-inch floppy disks, be sure also to fill out labels before you affix them to the disks. If you write on a label that is already on a disk, you can damage the disk if you press down too hard. If you must write on a label that is already on a disk, use a felt-tip pen, and write very gently. Do not apply pressure.

Write-Protect Your Disks

When you save files onto a disk, format a disk, or erase files from a disk, you can damage files if you make a mistake. If a disk is write-protected, you can read files on the disk, but you cannot save files on it, format it, or erase files from it. When you have an important disk that you want to protect the files on, write-protect it so that you do not inadvertently damage or delete files (Figure 4).

- When the write-protect notch on a 5¼-inch floppy disk is not covered, you can save, copy, and erase files on a disk. When the write-protect notch is

149

A. Data Disks

DATA DISK--ORIGINAL
Your Name / The Date
Formatted with DOS 4

DATA DISK--BACKUP
Your Name / The Date
Formatted with DOS 4

B. Program Disks

PROGRAM DISK--ORIGINAL
Your Name / The Date
Formatted with DOS 4

PROGRAM DISK--BACKUP
Your Name / The Date
Formatted with DOS 4

FIGURE 3   Disk Labels.   Disks labels should indicate the type of disk, whether it is an original or backup copy, your name, the date the disk was formatted, and the format used.

covered by tape, you cannot. You must use a write-protect tape that light cannot shine through since many drives use a light to determine if the notch is covered or not. If you use a transparent tape, the light will shine through the notch just as if it were not covered, and the drive will assume it is not write-protected.

- $3\frac{1}{2}$-inch floppy disks have a sliding tab that you press to open or close the write-protect window. When closed, you can save, copy, and erase files on a disk. When open, you cannot.

Backup Copies

Always make backup copies of your important files and disks, and save them a safe distance from your working area. Make sure the same accident cannot happen to both the original disk and its backup copy. The information on the disk is usually worth much more than the disk itself, so don't take chances. You can back

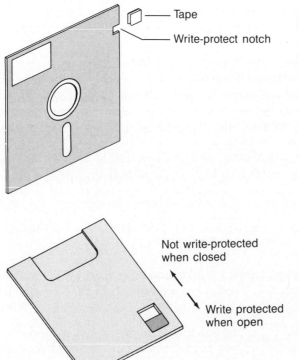

Tape

Write-protect notch

Not write-protected when closed

Write protected when open

FIGURE   4   Write-Protecting Floppy Disks.
A. Write-protecting a $5\frac{1}{4}$-inch disk
B. Write-protecting a $3\frac{1}{2}$-inch disk

up floppy disks using the Copy or Diskcopy commands described in Sec. 6 or 7, and hard disks using the Backup command described in the DOS manual.

Caring for Your Disks

Disks, both hard and floppy, are very reliable storage media. However, the data they contain can be lost or damaged if you do not take a few precautions. Floppy disks are relatively durable under ordinary conditions and have a useful life of about forty hours' spinning time. But that life can be shortened or abruptly ended by improper handling. Proper care ensures that disks will accurately store and play back the data you need.

Care of Hard Disk Drives

DON'T drop or jar them. They are very sensitive.

DO use the park program to move the drive's read/write head to a safe place on the disk before moving the computer.

Care of Floppy Disk Drives

DON'T use commercial cleaning kits too often. Overuse can cause problems with the drive.

DO insert the cardboard protectors that came with 5¼-inch disk drives and close the doors when moving the computer.

Care of Floppy Disks

DO keep disks in their protective storage envelopes. These envelopes reduce static buildup, which can attract dust that might scratch the disk.

DO keep disks dry, away from sneezes, coffee, or anything wet. A wet disk is a ruined disk.

DO prevent disks from getting too hot or too cold. They should be stored at temperatures of 50°–150°F (10°–52°C). Extremes of temperature can destroy a disk's sensitivity, so treat them the same way you treat photographic film; that is, keep them out of direct sunlight, do not leave them in a car exposed to temperature extremes, and so forth.

DO keep disks at least 2 feet away from magnets. The magnets found in copy stands, telephones, radio or stereo speakers, vacuum cleaners, televisions, air conditioners, novelty items, electric motors, or even some cabinet latches can ruin a disk's data.

DON'T touch a disk's recording surface. Handle them only by their protective covers.

DON'T use a hard-tipped pen to write on a disk label that is affixed to the disk. This can crease the disk inside the protective cover and cause you to lose data. Write on the label before affixing it to the disk, or use a felt-tip pen with very light pressure.

DON'T leave a disk in a nonoperating disk drive with the door closed for long periods. Open the drive door to lift the read/write head from the surface of the disk.

DON'T insert or remove a disk from the drive when the disk drive is running (that is, when the drive's light is on).

DON'T bend, fold, or crimp disks.

DON'T use paper clips to attach a floppy disk to a file folder or copy of a printout. Special folders are available that let you keep disks and printed documents together.

DON'T expose disks to static electricity. In dry climates or in heated buildings, static builds up when you walk on carpeted and some other kinds of floors. If you experience shocks when you touch metal objects, you are discharging the static that has built up. If you touch a disk when still charged with this static, you can damage the data. To prevent this, increase the humidity in the air, use static-proof carpets, or touch something like a typewriter to discharge the static before you pick up a disk.

Even with the best of care, floppy disks can last only so long. Close to the end of their useful life, they show their own form of senility by losing information or giving invalid commands. These are signs that it is time to replace the disk, which ideally, you have already made another backup copy of.

▼ 2. SPECIFYING DRIVES

CONCEPTS

When you first turn on your computer and load the operating system, drive A spins. If a disk in that drive contains the necessary operating system files, the operating system is loaded. Drive A operates because the computer's designers have placed a program in the computer's ROM telling it that it should address this drive when first turned on. Since it addresses drive A automatically, drive A is the default drive (Figure 5).

Although you cannot change the default drive that the computer addresses when you first turn it on, you can, and often do, copy, rename, delete, and save files from a drive other than the default drive. There are two ways to do this (Figure 6). You can change the default drive, or you can specify the other drive in the command.

Procedures

When working from the command prompt, you can quickly change the default drive by typing the letter of the drive and a colon (and an optional backslash) and then pressing ENTER. For example, if the default drive is set to A, and you want to change it to B, type **B:** or **B:** and then press ENTER. The command prompt indicates the current default drive. For example, *B>* or *B:\>* indicates that drive B is the default drive.

To specify a drive in a command, you enter the letters of the desired drives in the command followed by colons. For example, when you want to copy a file from drive A to drive B, you type the command **COPY A:FILENAME.EXT B:**.

FIGURE 5   The Default Drive.   The default drive is the drive the computer automatically addresses when you execute commands or copy files. It's like a model railroad where you can set a switch to send a train down one track or another.

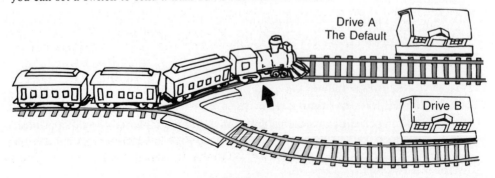

Drive A
The Default

Drive B

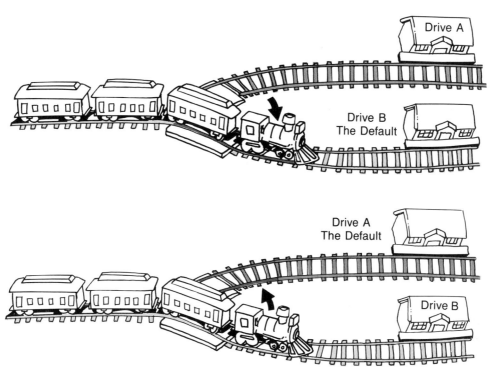

FIGURE 6   Addressing Another Drive.
A. You can change the default drive so that the program automatically addresses another drive rather than the original default drive. It's like changing the position of the switch on a model railroad to send the train down another track.
B. You can leave the default drive unchanged and specify another drive in your commands. This ignores the setting for the default drive and sends the command (or file if copying) to the drive that you specify. It's like sending a model train down a specified track regardless of how the switch is set.

When executing DOS's external commands, you have to specify drives in the commands. If the program is on the disk in the default drive, you have to type only its name to execute the command. Let's say you want to use the CHKDSK command to check a disk in drive B, and the operating system disk is in drive A. If the default drive is A, all you have to type is **CHKDSK B:**. But if the default drive is B, you have to type **A:CHKDSK B:**.

▼ 3. FORMATTING DATA DISKS

CONCEPTS

When you buy new blank disks to store your data or program files, you have to prepare them to run on your computer. This step is necessary because most disks are designed to be used on a wide variety of computers. Many computers and their operating systems use different methods to save files, so the blank disks must be customized for each type of system. This process is called formatting a disk.

The FORMAT command completely erases any data on a disk, so you should be careful. You should never format a previously used disk or a program disk unless you are sure you will not need any of the files on it. You also should never format a hard disk drive unless you are willing to lose every file on the disk. To see what files are on a disk before you format it, display the files on the disk as described in Sec. 4.

Procedures

To format a data disk from the command prompt, you use the FORMAT command. The FORMAT.COM file must be on one of the drives since this is an external command.

To Format a Data Disk from the Command Prompt

1. On a floppy disk system, insert the disk with the FORMAT.COM file into drive A and the disk to be formatted into drive B. Make drive A the default drive.

    On a hard disk system, insert the disk to be formatted into drive A. Make drive C the default drive.
2. Type **FORMAT B**: (on a floppy disk system) or **FORMAT A**: (on a hard disk system), and then press ENTER. The prompt reads *Insert new diskette for drive x: and press ENTER when ready*. (The *x* is the specified drive and varies depending on the system you are using.)
3. Since the disks were inserted in Step 1, press ENTER to continue. A message indicates the command's progress. In a few moments, a message reads *Format complete.*

    The status of the disk is displayed, and then a prompt reads *Format another (Y/N)?*.
4. Either press N and then press ENTER to quit formatting and return to the command prompt.

    Or insert a new disk into the same drive as you did in Step 1, press Y and then press ENTER to display the prompt asking you to insert a new disk. Press the designated key to continue.

▼ 4. ASSIGNING AND LISTING FILENAMES

CONCEPTS

When you save your work in files on a disk, the operating system uses filenames to keep track of individual files. In this topic, we introduce you to filenames and how to list the names of files on your disks.

Assigning Filenames

The files for the programs you use have already been assigned names. When you use these programs to create and save your own work, you must assign names to your files. The number and type of characters that you can use in a file's name are determined by the operating system you are using. For example, with DOS you can create filenames that have only eight characters and an optional period and three-character extension (Figure 7). The characters that are allowed are called legal characters and are listed in Table 1. Using any other character results in a name the computer will not accept.

TABLE 1   Characters That Can Be Used in Filenames

Characters	Examples
Letters	**A** through **Z** (uppercase or lowercase)
Numbers	**0** through **9**
Characters	! @ # $ % ^ & ( ) − _ { } ˜ ' `

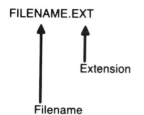

FILENAME.EXT

↑ Extension

↑ Filename

FIGURE 7 Filenames. File-names have two parts: the filename and an extension.

```
A:\>DIR

 Volume in drive A is RESOURCE
 Volume Serial Number is 3025-12EF
 Directory of  A:\

FILE1      TXT          19 01-01-80    4:31a
FILE3      TXT          17 02-20-89    1:47a
FILE5      TXT          17 02-20-89    1:47a
FILE6      TXT          17 01-30-91    1:48a
FILE7      TXT          17 01-30-91    1:49a
FILE8      TXT          17 01-30-91    1:49a
FILE9      TXT          17 01-30-91    1:49a
FILE10     TXT          18 01-30-91    1:49a
FILE11     TXT          18 01-30-91    1:50a
CHPT1      BAK        1024 01-30-91    1:50a
CHPT1      DOC        1024 01-30-91    1:51a
CHPT2      BAK        1024 01-30-91    1:51a
CHPT2      DOC        1024 01-30-91    1:51a
CHPT3      BAK        1024 01-30-91    1:52a
CHPT3      DOC        1024 01-30-91    1:52a
CHPT4      BAK        1024 01-30-91    1:52a
CHPT4      DOC        1024 01-30-91    1:52a
CHPT5      BAK        1024 01-30-91    1:52a
CHPT5      DOC        1024 01-30-91    1:52a
DBASE      BAT           9 01-30-91    1:54a
BUDGET91   WK1        5596 02-15-89    6:57p
WP5        BAT           7 01-30-91    1:54a
123        BAT           7 01-30-91    1:55a
BUDGET92   WK1        5596 02-15-89    6:58p
NAMES      BDF         982 02-15-89    7:00p
TEXTBOOK   DBF        1228 02-15-89    7:01p
README     BAT          10 01-30-91    2:02a
README     TXT          10 01-30-91    2:02a
FILE       TXT          18 01-01-80    1:36a
WHATSUP    DOC        9465 02-19-89   12:44p
GIVEUP     HUH        1051 02-19-89    6:55p
MYFILE     TXT         113 01-01-80    9:02p
EDIT       TXT         212 03-03-89    9:58a
BANKLOAN   WK1       12048 03-03-89   10:26a
BANKLOAN   PRN        3318 03-03-89   10:26a
FILELIST   BAT         117 01-01-80   10:12p
NAMES      DBF         982 02-15-89    7:00p
1-2-3            <DIR>     07-16-89    1:26p
DBASE            <DIR>     07-16-89    1:26p
WORD             <DIR>     07-16-89    1:26p
PLACEST    DBF        4676 08-08-89    9:44a
        44 File(s)     1384448 bytes free

A:\>
```

FIGURE 8 A Directory Displayed from the Command Prompt. Besides listing the filenames and their exten-sions, the DIR command also displays:
- The volume name
- The size of each file in bytes
- The date and time the file was last saved (useful only if you set the date and time each time you turn on the computer)
- The number of files on the disk
- How much free space is left on the disk

155

You can type filenames in uppercase letters, lowercase letters, or a combination of uppercase and lowercase. If you enter lowercase letters, the computer automatically converts them to uppercase on the disk.

Each filename you use must be unique if the file is not stored on a separate disk or in a separate directory on a hard disk drive (see Sec. 10). If you assign a file with the same name and extension as a file that is already on the disk, the new file will overwrite the previous file and erase it. However, you can use the same filename with different extensions, for example, LETTER.DOC and LETTER-.BAK. You can also use the same extension with different filenames.

Listing Files

Since a disk can hold many files, it is often necessary to find out what files are on a particular disk. The names of the files on a disk are held in a directory. To display this directory, you use the DIR command from the command prompt or display the DOS 4's File System.

PROCEDURES

With the operating command prompt on the screen, you can display filenames with the DIR command (Figure 8). If you do not specify a drive, the command lists the files on the default drive. To display the files in another drive, specify that drive in the command, for example:

- To list the files on the disk in drive A, type **DIR A:** and then press ENTER.
- To list the files on the disk in drive B, type **DIR B:** and then press ENTER.

If a list of files is too long to be displayed on the screen, some of the filenames will quickly scroll up and off the screen. Two commands prevent this: DIR/W or DIR B:/W and DIR/P or DIR B:/P. The /W and /P following the commands are parameters that modify the basic command.

- The /W parameter (for Wide) displays the filenames horizontally instead of vertically. This command drops the file size, date, and time information to make room for a horizontal listing of filenames. Because only the filenames are displayed and they are arranged horizontally on the screen, many filenames can be displayed on the screen at one time.
- The /P parameter (for Page) displays filenames until the screen is full. To display additional files, simply press any key. Since many screens can display only twenty-three filenames, this command is useful when more than twenty-three files are on a disk.

▼5. SPECIFYING FILES

CONCEPTS

In many operating system commands, you specify the name of a single file. Frequently, however, you want to work with groups of files. For example, when making a backup disk, you might want to copy all the files from one disk to another. Instead of working with one file at a time, you can work with several files at once.

Wildcards

When entering commands, you can specify groups of filenames using wildcards. A wildcard is simply a character that stands for one or more other characters, much like a wildcard in a card game. DOS wildcards are the question mark (?) and the asterisk (*).

FIGURE 9 The Question Mark Wildcard. The question mark wildcard stands for a specific character in the position of the question mark. In this figure, A shows the names of the files on a disk; B through E show and describe a series of commands with question mark wildcards and the files they display from the command prompt. The shaded character positions indicate the characters affected by the wildcards.

A. **????????.???** stands for the names of all files on the disk.
B. **BOO?.EXE** stands for any filename that has three or four characters and that begins with BOO followed by the extension .EXE.
C. **BO??.EXE** stands for any filename that has two to four characters and that begins with BO followed by the extension .EXE.
D. **B???.???** stands for any filename that has one to four characters and that begins with B followed by any extension of three or fewer characters.
E. **????.E??** stands for any filename that has four or fewer characters followed by any extension that begins with E.

A The Files on the Disk

?	?	?	?	?	?	?	?	.	?	?	?
B	O	O	T					.	E	X	E
B	O	O	K					.	E	X	E
B	O	R	E					.	E	X	E
B	A	D						.	P	R	T
B	O							.	D	O	C
L	O	V						.	E	X	
T	E	X	T					.			
T	E	X	T					.	1		
E	Y	E						.	D	O	C
W	O	R	D					.	C	H	6
N	A	M	E					.	L	S	T
R	E	A	D					.	M	E	
B	O	O	T					.	S	Y	S
B	O	T	T	L	E			.	D	O	C
B	R	A	I	N				.	E	X	E
B	Y	L	A	W	S			.	E	X	E
G	R	A	P	H	I	C	S	.	E	X	E
I	N	C	O	M	E			.	E	X	E

B The Command

B	O	O	?					.	E	X	E

The Results

B	O	O	T					.	E	X	E
B	O	O	K					.	E	X	E

C The Command

B	O	?	?					.	E	X	E

The Results

B	O	O	T					.	E	X	E
B	O	O	K					.	E	X	E
B	O	R	E					.	E	X	E

D The Command

B	?	?	?					.	?	?	?

The Results

B	O	O	T					.	E	X	E
B	O	O	K					.	E	X	E
B	O	R	E					.	E	X	E
B	A	D						.	P	R	T
B	O							.	D	O	C
B	O	O	T					.	S	Y	S

E The Command

?	?	?	?					.	E	?	?

The Results

B	O	O	T					.	E	X	E
B	O	O	K					.	E	X	E
B	O	R	E					.	E	X	E
L	O	V						.	E	X	

The Question Mark

The question mark can be used to substitute for any single character. If you think of all filenames fitting into a grid with eight columns for the filename and three columns for the extension, you can see how the question mark wildcard works (Figure 9).

The Asterisk

The asterisk is more powerful; it represents any character in a given position and all following characters. Again, if you think of all filenames fitting into a grid with eight columns for the filename and three columns for the extension, you can see how the asterisk wildcard works (Figure 10).

FIGURE 10 The Asterisk Wildcard. The asterisk wildcard stands for any group of characters from the position of the asterisk to the end of the filename or the end of the extension. In this figure, A shows the names of the files on a disk; B through D show and describe a series of commands with asterisk wildcards and the files they display. The shaded character positions indicate the characters affected by the wildcards.
A. ***.*** stands for any filename with any extension.
B. **B*.*** stands for any filename that begins with B followed by any extension.
C. **B*.EXE** stands for any filename that begins with B followed by the extension .EXE.
D. ***.E*** stands for any filename with an extension that begins with E.

A The Files on the Disk

*								.	*		
B	O	O	T					.	E	X	E
B	O	O	K					.	E	X	E
B	O	R	E					.	E	X	E
B	A	D						.	P	R	T
B	O							.	D	O	C
L	O	V						.	E	X	
T	E	X	T					.			
T	E	X	T					.	1		
E	Y	E						.	D	O	C
W	O	R	D					.	C	H	6
N	A	M	E					.	L	S	T
R	E	A	D					.	M	E	
B	O	O	T					.	S	Y	S
B	O	T	T	L	E			.	D	O	C
B	R	A	I	N				.	E	X	E
B	Y	L	A	W	S			.	E	X	E
G	R	A	P	H	I	C	S	.	E	X	E
I	N	C	O	M	E			.	E	X	E

B The Command

B	*							.	*		

The Results

B	O	O	T					.	E	X	E
B	O	O	K					.	E	X	E
B	O	R	E					.	E	X	E
B	A	D						.	P	R	T
B	O							.	D	O	C
B	O	O	T					.	S	Y	S
B	O	T	T	L	E			.	D	O	C
B	R	A	I	N				.	E	X	E
B	Y	L	A	W	S			.	E	X	E

C The Command

B	*							.	E	X	E

The Results

B	O	O	T					.	E	X	E
B	O	O	K					.	E	X	E
B	O	R	E					.	E	X	E
B	R	A	I	N				.	E	X	E
B	Y	L	A	W	S			.	E	X	E

D The Command

*								.	E	*	

The Results

B	O	O	T					.	E	X	E
B	O	O	K					.	E	X	E
B	O	R	E					.	E	X	E
B	R	A	I	N				.	E	X	E
B	Y	L	A	W	S			.	E	X	E
G	R	A	P	H	I	C	S	.	E	X	E
I	N	C	O	M	E			.	E	X	E

PROCEDURES

When working from the command prompt, you use the ? and * wildcards to specify groups of files. For example, to display all files with the extension .DOC, type **DIR *.DOC.** As you will see in the following topics, you can use these not only to display specific groups of files but also to copy, delete, and rename them.

 6. COPYING FILES

CONCEPTS

When you are working with files, you can copy them with the COPY command. This command copies one or more files from a disk in one drive to a disk in another drive. The COPY command is often used to make backup copies of important files.

When you use this command, you must specify three things:

1. Which disk they are to be copied from—the source disk
2. What is to be copied—the files
3. Which disk they are to be copied to—the target disk

▼ Source and Target Drives

When managing your files, you should understand the source and target drives.

The source is the drive containing the disk that you want the action performed on. The target is the drive containing the disk that you want to be affected by the source. For example, when you copy files from one disk to another, the disk you copy from is the source disk, and the disk you copy to is the target disk.

If you have only one floppy disk drive, specify the source drive as drive A and the target drive as drive B. The operating system will then prompt you to swap disks whenever it needs access to the source or target disk and it is not in the drive.

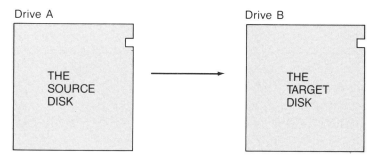

PROCEDURES

When you want a duplicate of one or more files, you use the COPY command. When you use this command from the command prompt, you can use wildcards to copy more than one file (see Sec. 4). Figure 11 shows some examples of how you use wildcards with the COPY command.

A Source Disk

F	I	L	E	N	A	M	E	.	E	X	T
F	1	L	E	1				.	D	O	C
F	I	L	E	2				.	D	O	C
F	I	L	E	3				.	D	O	C
M	A	N	U	A	L	1		.	D	O	C
F	1	L	E	1				.	B	A	K
F	I	L	E	2				.	B	A	K
F	I	L	E	3				.	B	A	K

Target Disk

F	I	L	E	1			.	D	O	C
F	I	L	E	2			.	D	O	C
F	I	L	E	3			.	D	O	C

B Source Disk

F	I	L	E	N	A	M	E	.	E	X	T
F	1	L	E	1				.	D	O	C
F	I	L	E	2				.	D	O	C
F	I	L	E	3				.	D	O	C
M	A	N	U	A	L	1		.	D	O	C
F	1	L	E	1				.	B	A	K
F	I	L	E	2				.	B	A	K
F	I	L	E	3				.	B	A	K

Target Disk

F	I	L	E	1			.	D	O	C
F	I	L	E	2			.	D	O	C
F	I	L	E	3			.	D	O	C
F	1	L	E	1			.	B	A	K
F	I	L	E	2			.	B	A	K
F	I	L	E	3			.	B	A	K

C Source Disk

F	1	L	E	1			.	D	O	C
F	I	L	E	2			.	D	O	C
F	I	L	E	3			.	D	O	C
M	A	N	U	A	L	1	.	D	O	C
L	O	T	U	S			.	B	A	T
W	P						.	B	A	T

Target Disk

L	O	T	U	S		.	B	A	T
W	P					.	B	A	T

D Source Disk

F	1	L	E	1			.	D	O	C
F	I	L	E	2			.	D	O	C
F	I	L	E	3			.	D	O	C
M	A	N	U	A	L	1	.	D	O	C
L	O	T	U	S	,		.	B	A	T
W	P						.	B	A	T

Target Disk

F	1	L	E	1			.	D	O	C
F	I	L	E	2			.	D	O	C
F	I	L	E	3			.	D	O	C
M	A	N	U	U	A	S	L	1	.	D	O	C
L	O	T	U	S			.	B	A	T
W	P						.	B	A	T

E Target Disk

F	I	L	E	N	A	M	E	.	E	X	T
F	1	L	E	1				.	D	O	C
F	I	L	E	2				.	D	O	C
F	I	L	E	3				.	D	O	C
M	A	N	U	A	L	1		.	D	O	C
F	1	L	E	1				.	B	A	K
F	I	L	E	2				.	B	A	K
F	I	L	E	3				.	B	A	K

Source Disk

F	I	L	E	N	A	M	E	.	E	X	T
F	1	L	E	1				.	D	O	C
F	I	L	E	2				.	D	O	C
F	I	L	E	3				.	D	O	C
M	A	N	U	A	L	1		.	D	O	C
F	1	L	E	1				.	B	A	K
F	I	L	E	2				.	B	A	K
F	I	L	E	3				.	B	A	K

FIGURE 11   **Using Wildcards to Copy Files from Drive A to Drive B.**   When you use wildcards to copy files from one disk to another, the wildcards affect the files that are copied. In the examples shown here, the shaded character positions indicate the characters affected by the wildcards.

A. **COPY A:FILE?.DOC B:** will copy all files on drive A named FILE followed by any single character and an extension .DOC to drive B.

B. **COPY A:FILE?.* B:** will copy all files on drive A named FILE followed by any single character and any extension to drive B.

C. **COPY A:*.BAT B:** will copy all files on drive A having the extension .BAT to drive B.

D. **COPY A:*.* B:** will copy all files on drive A to drive B.

E. **COPY B:*.* A:** will copy all files on drive B to drive A.

160

To copy one or more files, you must specify the source and target drives in the COPY command only if they are not the default drives, for example:

- If the default drive is set to A, and you want to copy a file named LETTER on drive A to drive B, you would type **COPY LETTER B:**. This command reads "copy the file named LETTER in the default drive to drive B." You do not need to specify drive A because that is the default drive. If you did, you would type **COPY A:LETTER B:**.
- If the default drive is set to B, and you want to copy a file named LETTER on drive A to drive B, you would type **COPY A:LETTER**. The command reads "copy the file named LETTER in drive A to the default drive." You do not need to specify drive B because that is the default drive.
- Regardless of which drive is the default, you can specify both the source and target drives as a precaution. For example, to copy the file named LETTER from drive A to drive B regardless of which drive is the default drive, type **COPY A:LETTER B:**. This command reads "copy the file named LETTER in drive A to drive B."

To Copy Files from Drive A to Drive B from the Command Prompt

1. Insert the source disk into drive A and the target disk into drive B.
2. Type **A:** and then press ENTER to change the default drive to drive A.
3. Either type **COPY *.* B:** and then press ENTER to copy all files.

   Or type the file's name, and then press ENTER to copy a single file.
4. Repeat Steps 1 through 3 for each disk that you want to copy. (Remember, you can press F3 and then ENTER to repeat the COPY command.)

7. DUPLICATING DISKS

CONCEPTS

As you have seen, you can use the COPY command with wildcards to copy all the files from one disk to another to make a backup copy. The DISKCOPY command (an external command) also lets you make a backup copy of a floppy disk. So why are there two commands to do the same thing?

- The DISKCOPY command does not require you to format the disk you are copying the files to. The DISKCOPY command automatically formats the disk before it begins to copy the files. You cannot use this command to copy files to a disk that already contains files unless you want to erase the existing files.
- The COPY command does not make an exact duplicate of a disk. It copies the files but not their exact location on the disk. When you want to make an exact duplicate of a disk, use the DISKCOPY command. If a disk is full and files are stored in noncontiguous sectors, it takes the drive longer to save and retrieve them. The COPY *.* command will copy them so that they are all on contiguous sectors, but the DISKCOPY command will not. If you are making backup copies, it is better to use the COPY *.* command.

PROCEDURES

To duplicate a disk from the command prompt, insert the operating system disk that contains the DISKCOPY.COM file into drive A, type **DISKCOPY A: B:** and then press ENTER. A prompt asks you to insert the source and target disks. Insert the source disk (the one you are copying from) into drive A. (Write-protect it so that you do not inadvertently erase it.) Insert the target disk (the one you are copying to) into drive B, and then press any key to continue. When the first disk is duplicated, a prompt asks if you want to duplicate more. Press the specified keys to quit or continue.

To Duplicate a Disk in Drive A to Drive B from the Command Prompt

1. On a floppy disk system, insert the DOS disk that contains the DISKCOPY-.COM file into drive A, and then make that the default drive. On a hard disk system, make drive C the default drive.
2. Type **DISKCOPY A: B:** and then press ENTER. You are prompted to insert the source and target disks. (On a hard disk system with a single floppy disk drive, you are only prompted to insert the source disk.)
3. On a floppy disk system, insert the source disk (the one being duplicated) into drive A, and insert the target disk (the duplicate) into drive B.

    On a hard disk system, insert the source disk into drive A. Remove it, and then replace it with the target disk when prompted to do so.

    When ready, press any key to continue. A message indicates the sectors and tracks being copied. In a few moments, the prompt reads *Copy another diskette (Y/N)?*.
4. Either insert the new disk(s) into the same drive(s) as you did in Step 3, press Y and then press any key to duplicate additional disks.

    Or   press N to stop and return to the command prompt.

8. RENAMING FILES

CONCEPTS

There are times when you want to change the name of a file on a disk. To do this, you use the RENAME or REN commands (internal commands).

PROCEDURES

To rename files from the command prompt, you use the RENAME command (an internal command). You can also use REN, a shorter version of the command, to do the same thing. When using this command from the command prompt, you must specify the old name and the new name. You can add specify a path for the source but not for the target name. For example, when the *A>* command prompt is on the screen, and a disk in drive B has a file named OLDNAME.EXT that you want to change to NEWNAME.EXT, you type **RENAME B:OLDNAME.EXT NEWNAME.EXT** and then press ENTER.

9. DELETING FILES

CONCEPTS

Monitoring the amount of free space on a disk is important because many applications programs misbehave when you ask them to save files on a full disk, or they may create temporary files that take up a lot of space. Most people tend to keep files long after they are useful. It is good practice to occasionally use the File System or DIR command to list the files on a disk and then delete any files no longer needed.

PROCEDURES

When you want to delete one or more files, you use the ERASE or DEL command. These two commands are interchangeable and work exactly alike. For example, with the *A*> command prompt on the screen, and a disk in drive B that you want to delete a file named FILENAME.EXT from, you type **ERASE B: FILENAME.EXT** or **DEL B:FILENAME.EXT** and then press ENTER.

You can use wildcards with the ERASE and DEL commands, but it is dangerous to do so. Miscalculating even slightly the effects that wildcards have can cause the wrong files to be deleted. However, there are precautions you can take:

- One way to use wildcards safely is to preview which files will be affected by specifying the planned wildcards with the DIR command. If only the files you want to delete are listed, the same wildcards are safe to use with the ERASE or DEL command. For example, if you want to delete all files with the extension .BAK, type **DIR *.BAK.** If the list of files can all be deleted, type **DEL *.BAK.**
- To be prompted for each file when using DOS 4, use the /P parameter. For example, to delete all files with the extension .BAK, type **DEL *.BAK/P.** Before each file is deleted, a prompt reads *Delete (Y/N)?*. Press Y to delete the file, or press N to leave the file on the disk.
- If you use the *.* wildcards, a prompt reads *Are you sure (Y/N)?*. Press Y to continue and delete all the files, or press N to cancel the command.

To Delete Files from a Disk from the Command Prompt

1. Select the name of the file(s) you want to delete. (If you plan on using wildcards, preview the results of the ERASE or DEL command by typing **DIR** followed by a filename. Use the ? wildcard to stand for a specific character or the * wildcard to stand for any group of characters.)
2. Type **ERASE** or **DEL** followed by the name of the file to be deleted. (If using wildcards, use the ones you entered to preview the results.)
3. Press ENTER to delete the files.

▼ 10. USING DIRECTORIES

CONCEPTS

When using DOS, you can divide a hard (or floppy) disk into directories, which help you organize files on these disks. Imagine if you used a file drawer to store all of your memos, letters, and reports. Before long, the drawer would become so crowded that you could not find anything. But with a little organization and planning, the documents could be organized into folders, making it easier to locate the needed document (Figure 12).

A hard disk is like an empty drawer in a new filing cabinet: It provides a lot of storage space but no organization (Figure 13). To make it easier to find items in the drawer, you can divide it into categories with hanging folders. You can file

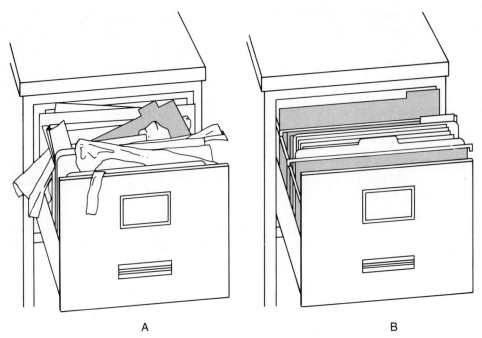

A   B

FIGURE 12   File Drawers.   Unorganized file drawers make it difficult to find files when you need them (a). Organized file drawers make it easy to find the files you want (b).

documents directly into the hanging folders, or you can divide them into finer categories with manila folders. A directory is like a hanging folder, and a subdirectory is like a manila folder within a hanging folder. A file in a directory or subdirectory is like a letter, report, or other document within either a hanging folder or a manila folder.

Directories on a hard disk drive are organized in a hierarchy (Figure 14). The main directory, the one not below any other directory, is the root directory. Below it, directories can be created on one or more levels. These directories can hold files or subdirectories.

PROCEDURES

Any disk may be divided into directories and subdirectories. You will often find floppy disks with directories, and almost every hard disk has them. To work with these disks, you have to know how to move around through the directories and display the names of files that you want to work with.

Changing Directories

To change directories from the command prompt, you use the CHDIR or CD command. To change the default directory, type **CD** then type the name of the drive and directory, and then press ENTER. If you are changing more than one level, list the directories in order, separated by a backslash. For example, to change to a directory named OLD that is a subdirectory of a directory named LETTERS, type **CD\LETTERS\OLD**. There are several versions of these commands; for example, in Figure 15:

A. To make the subdirectory OLD the default directory, you type **CD\LET-TERS\OLD** and then press ENTER.
B. To move up one directory, for example, from OLD to LETTERS, you type **CD..** and then press ENTER.

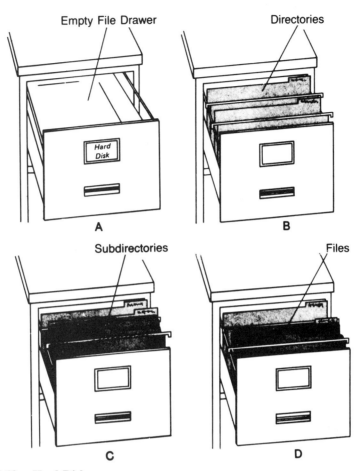

FIGURE 13   Hard Disks.
A. A new hard disk is like an empty file drawer. It has lots of room for files but no organization.
B. You can divide the hard disk into directories, which is like dividing the file drawer with hanging folders.
C. You can then subdivide the directories into smaller subdirectories, which is like dividing the hanging folders with manila folders.
D. You can then save files in any of these subdirectories the same way you would file a document in one of the manila folders.

C. To move down to a subdirectory within the current directory, type **CD** press SPACEBAR then type the name of the directory, and then press ENTER. For example, to change from LETTERS to NEW, you type **CD NEW.**

D. To return to the root directory from any other directory, you type **CD** and then press ENTER.

To display the default directory on the current drive, type **CD** and then press ENTER. To display the current default directory on another drive, type **CD** followed by the drive identifier, and then press ENTER. For example, to display the current directory on drive C, type **CD C:** and then press ENTER.

Displaying Files

When you want a list of your hard disk's organization, you use the TREE command (an external command) (Figure 16). When you want a list of the directories, and the files they contain, you use the /F parameter, for example, TREE/F (Figure 17). This command, unlike the DIR command, lists files in all directories.

165

Root Directory ⟶

Directories ⟶

Subdirectories ⟶

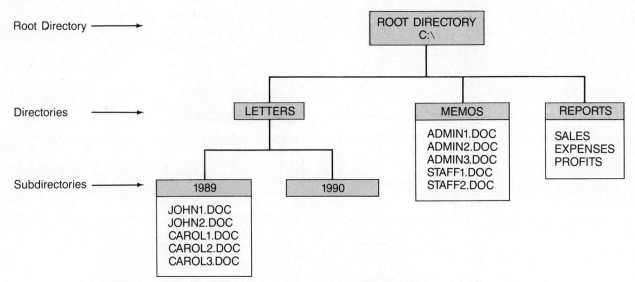

FIGURE 14   Directory Trees.   On the hard disk, directories and subdirectories are organized into a treelike hierarchy. The topmost directory is called the root directory. Directories below it are called directories. When directories are subdivided into additional directories, they are called subdirectories.

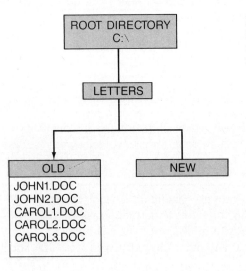

FIGURE 15   Moving Through Directories.   This tree shows the root directory, a LETTERS directory, and two subdirectories.

```
Directory PATH listing for Volume RESOURCE
Volume Serial Number is 09F8-0958
```

FIGURE 16   The TREE Command.   The TREE command lists just the directories on the disk.

```
Directory PATH listing for Volume RESOURCE
Volume Serial Number is 09F8-0958
B:.
    │   FILE1.TXT
    │   FILE2.TXT
    │   FILE3.TXT
    │   FILE4.TXT
    │   FILE5.TXT
    │   FILE6.TXT
    │   FILE7.TXT
    │   FILE8.TXT
    │   FILE9.TXT
    │   FILE10.TXT
    │   FILE11.TXT
    │   CHPT1.BAK
    │   CHPT1.DOC
    │   CHPT2.BAK
    │   CHPT2.DOC
    │   CHPT3.BAK
    │   CHPT3.DOC
    │   CHPT4.BAK
    │   CHPT4.DOC
    │   CHPT5.BAK
    │   CHPT5.DOC
    │   BUDGET91.WK1
    │   BUDGET92.WK1
    │   NAMELIST.DBF
    │   PUBLISH.DBF
    │   README.BAT
    │   README.TXT
    │   FILE.TXT
    │
    ├───1-2-3
    │   │   README.TXT
    │   │
    │   └───OLD
    │           README.TXT
    │
    ├───DBASE
    │       README.TXT
    │
    └───WORD
            README.TXT
```

FIGURE 17 The TREE/F Command. The TREE/F command lists directories and files on the disk.

To List Directories and Files from the Command Prompt

- To display a list of directories, type **TREE** and then press ENTER.
- To display a list of directories and the files they contain, type **TREE/F** and then press ENTER.

▼ 11. MAKING AND REMOVING DIRECTORIES

CONCEPTS

When you want to organize your work on a hard disk drive, you create directories. When the directories are no longer needed, you remove them (after deleting all the files they contain).

When creating directories, you should have some kind of a plan. It makes sense to follow these rules:

- Keep only essential files, like AUTOEXEC.BAT and CONFIG.SYS, in the root directory.

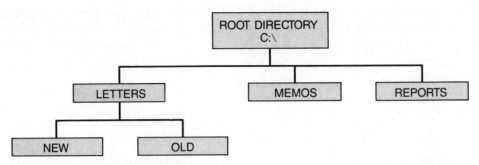

FIGURE 18   Making Directories.   This tree shows the root directory, a LETTERS directory, and two subdirectories.

- Store all program files related to a program in their own directory. For example, you might want a directory for DOS, 1-2-3, WordPerfect, and dBASE.
- Do not store the data files that you create in the same directory as the program files. Keep all related data files in their own directories. For example, you might have separate directories for letters, reports, financial documents, and name and address lists. You might also create separate directories for the files you create with different programs. For example, you might have separate directories for WordPerfect documents, 1-2-3 worksheets, or dBASE database files.
- Do not create too many levels since it takes time to move around them. Most disks can be well organized with no more than three levels, including the root directory.

When creating and deleting directories, here are some rules to keep in mind:

- When you create directories, you assign them names. These names follow the same conventions that you use for filenames. However, you should not use a period and extension, or you might confuse directories with filenames at some later date. Files and subdirectories in one directory can have the same names as files and subdirectories in other directories.
- Before you can remove a directory, you must delete all the files it contains. If the directory contains subdirectories, you must first also delete the files they contain, and then delete the subdirectories.
- You cannot delete the current directory or the root directory.
- You can create as many directories and subdirectories as you want, but the path (see Sec. 12) cannot exceed sixty-three characters.

PROCEDURES

To make a directory from the command prompt, you type **MKDIR** (or **MD**) followed by the name of the directory you are creating. The form of the command depends on whether you are working in the directory off of which you want to create a directory or subdirectory. For example, if you wanted to create the directories shown in Figure 18, you type:

- **MD\LETTERS** and then press ENTER
- **MD\MEMOS** and then press ENTER
- **MD\REPORTS** and then press ENTER

To make the two subdirectories off the LETTERS directory, you type:

- **MD\LETTERS\NEW** and then press ENTER
- **MD\LETTERS\OLD** and then press ENTER

If you first changed directories so that LETTERS was the default directory, you could create the two subdirectories by typing:

- **MD NEW** and then pressing ENTER
- **MD OLD** and then pressing ENTER

To Create Directories from the Command Prompt

- To create a directory off the root directory regardless of the directory you are in, type **MD** followed by the name of the directory.
- To create a directory off the root directory of another drive, type **MD** followed by the drive identifier, a slash, and the directory name.
- To create a subdirectory in the current directory, type **MD** followed by the directory name.

Removing Directories

To remove a directory from the command prompt, you must first delete all the files that it contains. Next, you have to move to the directory above the one to be removed. To do so, type **CD..** and then press ENTER. Now, type **RMDIR** (or **RD**) followed by the name of the directory you are removing. If you want to remove a directory that contains subdirectories, you must first remove the subdirectories. You cannot delete the current default directory from the command prompt.

12. SPECIFYING PATHS

CONCEPTS

In previous topics, you frequently specified drives when executing commands that copied, moved, or deleted files on disks. When a disk is divided into directories, you not only must specify a drive, you also must specify a directory in many commands. Specifying the drive and directories is called specifying a path.

Paths are instructions to the program that tell it what subdirectory a file is located in or where it should be placed. It is like telling someone that "the letter to ACME Hardware is in the manila folder labeled ACME in the hanging folder labeled Hardware in the third file cabinet from the right." These precise instructions make it easy to locate the file.

Paths are simply a listing of the directories and subdirectories between where a file is and where you are or want the file to be copied to. To specify a path, you must indicate:

1. The drive
2. The name of the directory (or directories)
3. The filename

PROCEDURES

To specify a path from the command prompt, you must indicate the drive, then the name of all subdirectories, and then the filename. All elements must be separated from one another by backslashes (\), for example, C:\LETTER\NEW\FILE-1.DOC. When copying or moving files from the DOS 4 Shell's File System, you have to specify only a path to the target directory in the *To:* field of the Copy or Move pop-up.

When specifying paths from the command prompt, you have to consider both the source and target directories:

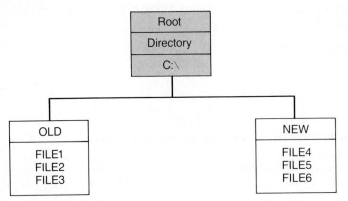

FIGURE 19   Default Directories and Paths When Copying or Moving Files. This figure shows the root directory and two subdirectories.

- If the source directory is the default, you have to specify only the path to the target.
- If the target directory is the default, you have to specify only the path to the source.
- If neither the target nor the source directory is the default, you have to specify the path for both.

For example, let's assume your disk has the directories and files shown in Figure 19.

- When copying or moving files from the command prompt, you have to specify a path only when the source or target directory is not the default.
  - When OLD is the default, the path you specify to copy FILE1 to the NEW directory is specified only for the target. For example, from the command prompt, you type **COPY FILE1 C:\NEW.**
  - When NEW is the default, the path you specify to copy FILE1 to the NEW directory is specified only for the source. For example, from the command prompt, you type **COPY C:\OLD\FILE1.**
  - When the root directory is the default, the paths you specify to copy FILE1 to the NEW directory are for both the source and the target. For example, from the command prompt, you type **COPY C:\OLD\FILE1 C:\OLD.**
- When you want to display a list of the filenames in a directory, the same principles work.
  - When the root directory is the default, you can display its directory by just typing **DIR** and then pressing ENTER.
  - To display the files in the OLD directory, you type **DIR C:\OLD** and then press ENTER.
  - To display the files in the NEW directory, you type **DIR C:\NEW** and then press ENTER.
- When you want to delete a file, the same principles work. For example, when OLD is the default directory:
  - To delete FILE1, you type **DEL FILE1** and then press ENTER.
  - To delete FILE4, you type **DEL C:\NEW\FILE4** and then press ENTER.

Index